RESTORING BROKEN TRUST

A relationship's greatest challenge

MARK BEAIRD

iUniverse LLC
Bloomington

Restoring Broken Trust
A relationship's greatest challenge

iUniverse books may be ordered through booksellers or by contacting:

iUniverse LLC
1663 Liberty Drive
Bloomington, IN 47403
www.iuniverse.com
1-800-Authors (1-800-288-4677)

ISBN: 978-1-4917-1231-3 (sc)
ISBN: 978-1-4917-1232-0 (e)

Printed in the United States of America.

iUniverse rev. date: 10/31/2013

CONTENTS

· · · · · ·

Acknowledgments vii

Introduction ix

Chapter 1   Why Trust is Broken 1

Chapter 2   How Trust is Broken 14

Chapter 3   Forgiveness and Trust 26

Chapter 4   The Nature of Forgiveness 35

Chapter 5   The Nature of Trust 49

Chapter 6   Committed to the Process 64

Chapter 7   Our Initial Response to the Hurt 72

Chapter 8   Admitting One's Guilt 79

Chapter 9   To Whom the Confession is Being Made 91

Chapter 10 Now that the Door is Open 105

Chapter 11 It's Time to Prove Yourself 117

Chapter 12 Tough Questions Remain 132

Chapter 13 What Does a Healthy, Trusting Relationship
            Look Like? 146

Chapter 14 Learning to Connect in a Healthy Way 159

Chapter 15   Learning to Trust Again 168

Chapter 16   Keep Your Goal in Sight 185

Chapter 17   Closure the Payoff for Doing the Work................. 197

Chapter 18   Closing Thoughts...204

Appendix 213

Works Cited.. 217

Recommended Reading by Category 225

About the Author..229

ACKNOWLEDGMENTS

· · · · · ·

T he older I get, and especially working in the field of counseling, the more I realize what a blessing having good parents and a good family has been in my life. My father passed away a number of years ago, but I still have my mother Doris, who is a treasure to me. When I was growing up, she was always there to sit and talk with me, to listen to my feelings and thoughts, and to instill an empathetic heart in me. She would have made a great counselor. If I am ever a good counselor, or if I am able to help someone, my mother will deserve part of the credit. Her taking the time to instill in me a sense of empathy was a priceless gift. I owe her a measure of gratitude not easy to express.

Thank you to Brenda Kay Coulter for her editorial work, to friends like Rue Dene Sasser, Bill Coffey, Marie Brewer, David Mullins, and Dr. Oliver McMahan, for their insight on the content and help with proofing.

It is my hope that in some small way, this book will help people clearly see the right path to take in developing or in restoring the trust in their relationships.

INTRODUCTION

. . . . . .

B roken trust between people takes place in a variety of ways and the closer the relationship the more devastating it can be. Often it is so upsetting because of the affect it has on the relationship and the surrounding relationships. Broken trust in relationships may take the form of an extramarital affair that brings a couple to the point of intense anguish and threatens to dissolve the marriage. In other instances, it is the revelation of dishonest business dealings from a trusted colleague or business partner. Far too often the problem of broken trust stems from a family, parent, or spouse dealing with addictions. I have never dealt with an individual who struggled with addiction—be it drugs, alcohol, gambling, sex, or other vices—that had not woven a web of lies and deception in an attempt to conceal the addictive behavior. Then there is the common but hurtful act of betraying someone's confidence or failing to follow through on an important promise. It could happen in various ways, but lying for one reason or another is not unheard of among human beings. It's a common occurrence. Just the same, although it may be common, it doesn't hurt any less.

Lastly, there are instances of broken trust that fall into the category of emotional hurt that does not necessarily involve lying or even deceitfulness. These breaks in trust come from harsh or hurtful words or actions or a person failing another in a significant way due to apparent carelessness or lack of consideration. In other instances, one person constantly leaves the other person emotionally off balance by threatening to leave the other. As someone described it, "They're always living with one foot out the door." Either way, when a person experiences this type of behavior he often feels he can no longer trust that person not to hurt him, abandon him, or fail him in the future. The party in question never lied, never tried to deceive, but was simply so self-absorbed the other person was never really considered in a caring way. Therefore, the trust has been broken. Confidence in that person is lost.

Webster's Dictionary defines *trust* as: *a.* "an assured reliance on the character, ability, strength, or truth of someone or something; *b*: one in which confidence is placed." By definition trust is an awesome trait in a relationship that is filled with weighty expectations. Yet, when that "assured reliance" fails, everything we have tried to build or hoped for seems to come crashing down and lies broken in pieces at our feet. It feels like, to paraphrase the old childhood nursery rhyme, Humpty Dumpty, "All the king's horses and all the king's men can't put the relationship back together again."

However, in this case, feelings only become reality if we fail to challenge them—and challenge them we must. In spite of what some may say, many times—though not always—broken trust can be restored and relationships can be saved. Yes, there are times when we should not continue a relationship. For instance, if being in that relationship would result in being physically or emotionally abused, I would never advise trying to make it work, but that type of mistreatment is not our focus in this book.

In addition, as you read the following pages it is important to remember that everyone does not intend to be dishonest. Not everyone is intentionally deceptive, but it's a fine line between, *I wasn't thinking how that would look or sound . . .* and, *It won't hurt to bend the truth a little.* Yes, wrong is still wrong. Nevertheless, sometimes it is relevant and helpful when we see the hurt was not premeditated, and initially, any hope is welcome. For the time being, just consider the possibility that people can and do change for the better, and the pain of broken trust can go away if we allow the hurt to heal. We will talk more about how that can happen later.

There are several essential elements to rebuilding trust in a relationship, but it can be difficult to know where to begin because people are often at different places in their relationships. Consequently, each person is seeking answers for where they have found themselves and for what they are presently encountering. Therefore, we must choose a starting point, and for me I would like us to begin with forgiveness. Before I finish, I will have circled back several times continuing to touch on forgiveness because it is a key component to rebuilding broken trust and the broken relationship. It may seem that other components would be more important, but remember, the only person you can control is yourself and forgiveness is one of those things over which you have control. For now, let's begin by trying to answer some questions concerning how relationships get to the point of needing restoration.

CHAPTER ONE

Why Trust is Broken

· · · · · ·

The "why" and "how" of trust being broken is difficult to separate because in many instances we are talking about the same type of behavior. Yet, for the sake of trying to bring clarity to the subject, allow me to discuss both. This will help me build the foundation of my case in favor of trying to rebuild the trust in broken relationships. I begin here because trying to understand people before we judge them, criticize them, or try to rebuild a relationship with them will eventually affect the forgiveness we offer to them and the nature of the relationship we will ultimately choose with them.

With this in mind I submit to you that the question of, "Why is trust broken?" differs somewhat from the question of "How is trust broken?" first because it questions the motive, the personality, or the nature of the person who has broken our trust. On the other hand, the question of "How is trust broken?" calls into question the actual behavior in which one is engaged at the time of his/her breaking another person's trust. It is important to consider both because at times people break the trust of another intentionally and sometimes unintentionally.

Furthermore, at times the break in trust is the result of an eroding process in which trust is worn away by numerous events over the years and not by one specific event like infidelity. I do not mean to make it sound complicated, just to address our tendency to think in a black-and-white or all-or-nothing state of mind. It is what Aaron Beck called "Polarized Thinking" when he first proposed a list of what he referred to as "cognitive distortions"—later made popular by David Burns in his book, *Feeling Good: The new mood therapy.* This "polarized" way of thinking eliminates all middle ground. It does not allow for complicated situations often found in misunderstandings between people. Again, we are only venturing down this path to make sure we have a thorough grasp of the situation before we proceed. We are not building a case for excusing wrongdoing.

With this in mind, consider a few general reasons *why* trust is often broken in relationships.

Misguided Assumptions

One relational truth is certain: If you and I live long enough we will eventually find ourselves being disappointed in someone and someone will eventually be disappointed in us. It may not be anything major like a moral failure, but at some point someone who has been disappointed in us will say, "But I thought you . . . would . . . were going to . . . had already . . ." You get the point. We have most likely uttered those words to someone or about someone. Someone let us down and we find ourselves saying, "But I thought for sure I could depend on him" or "I thought for sure she was telling me the truth."

What is happening in these instances is that we have, or they have, made assumptions about the intent or integrity of another. With an assumption, we are taking for granted something is true without verifying it. We presumed and yes, we assumed. Any way we want to say it, we thought one thing or another. But we were wrong, or they were. The problem is people do not think as much as we think they think. We are making all these assumptions about the other person and his behavior, and yet we have said nothing to the person to clarify that we are on the same page.

Granted, many times when someone breaks our trust, or we theirs, it was done with at least some intent, but it is not always the case. Clearly, we are not talking about a marital affair or someone embezzling funds from a company or another obvious breach in trust. Just the same, many relationships in families and among friends have gone sour because of what was essentially a misunderstanding, but someone insisted it was intentional.

Allow me to give you an absurd example—at least it was absurd from my perspective. It was a number of years ago when I was a young pastor. It seems a woman in my church had lost confidence in me because, in her mind, I didn't care about her as one of my church members. The woman in question came to church every Sunday morning, but never any other time. That was her routine. One Sunday she showed up being upset with me because she had been in the hospital during the week and I had not come to see her. I asked if she had told me. Had I forgotten? "No," she replied. "Did you tell anyone else?" "No," she answered. Understand, she never broke from her routine, never told anyone she was sick, never told anyone she was going in the hospital, and never told any of her family to let me know. Yet, in her mind, I didn't care about her or else I would have come to the hospital! You're kidding me. Really?

There have been times I thought I was having a psychotic episode, but I have never had a psychic episode. Did she think I was connected telepathically to everyone who was a member of my church? Yet, in her mind, I was a terrible pastor who didn't care. That is absurd! Can I get an amen?

Even as bizarre as that example is, I have seen couples and families at odds with one another even though the hurt was a matter of misguided assumptions on the part of someone. The perspective seems to be, "Well, they should know better." Well, obviously they didn't. Plaintiffs usually have to be coaxed into admitting that "maybe" they could have been clearer in stating their expectations or directions—I would say, at least as clear as they were in their condemnation of the other party for being morally defective.

Questionable Character

Now, let us proceed with a look at why trust is often broken. We will begin with the nature of some people. Often I see trust broken by people known for disregarding the rights of others. These people often see a boundary like the proverbial "line in the sand" as nothing more than an inconvenience. These individuals continually show—despite what they say—that they really don't care about others' feelings.

John was the type of fellow we have in mind. He was smart, confident to the point of being cocky, and could be charming when he wanted to be. Nevertheless, his wife had noticed after only a couple years of marriage that John didn't appear to show any true compassion for other people. He appeared as if he didn't care about the feelings of others. Anything he did at work or in his personal dealings with others that looked dishonest was quickly explained away or justified. Essentially, he did what he wanted when he wanted and didn't feel bad about others being hurt or inconvenienced by his behavior.

John could have, and did, break the trust of others in many different ways, but it was not the result of not knowing the rules of human civility; rather it was his personality or character to disregard them altogether. Lecturing him on the rules was a waste of breath. The problem wasn't knowledge, it was nature.

Joe was similar in many ways, yet different. Joe would break the rules of mutual respect as well, but he did so simply because he was better than everyone else—at least in his own mind. From his perspective, there was always a good reason for his behavior, but it was always be traced back to the apparent belief he was different or unique from other people. To question him was to suffer the brunt of his anger as he indignantly defended his actions through long, drawn-out "discussions" in which he would discuss the stupidity of the other's perspective and he or she would listen.

To put it mildly, Joe felt entitled—entitled to have whatever or to do whatever he thought or wanted. He might try charm to persuade others or to get his way. He might use his supposedly superior logic. It wasn't even beneath him to pout or sulk; but clearly he always expected compliance with his wishes. Consequently, when he did not feel his wife was admiring and appreciative enough of him, he felt entitled to treat her any way he chose and eventually reward a more adoring woman with his affection.

These are but a couple of fictional, though all too real, examples of the way a person's questionable character can influence his behavior and the way he justifies that same behavior. In both accounts of John and Joe, both were more than willing to break the trust of others with ease. It was their nature. Why couldn't they see the other person's perspective? They didn't even really try. Sadly, the other person was irrelevant. It wasn't that they thought, "I know this could hurt _____ but I'm going to do it anyway." It was that they never thought of them at all. Yes, that is difficult for most to comprehend, but it is part of the answer to, "Why?"

Poor Boundaries and Unclear Expectations

Often I see good people who lack wisdom in relationships. It's not like they have not had bad experiences in the past from which they could have learned something. In fact, their past is scattered with hurtful relationships. Sometimes, this is due to the person's unmet emotional needs clouding the person's judgment. It may be a dysfunctional pattern of behavior that has developed over time, or copied from a parent, or family member, who lacked healthy boundaries or who never placed expectations on others. In other words, people were free to treat them as they chose.

A good example of someone primed to be disappointed with people in this way is the person who is constantly dismayed that others continue to hurt her. She is so sensitive, gives her heart so freely, and bends over backwards trying to please others with whom she is in a relationship. She is never, and I mean never, the source of hurtful words or actions. Yet, others continually seem to hurt her and she is left in a puddle of tears wondering what went wrong.

That was the situation with Carter and Louise. Carter was, and had always been, all about Carter. Louise was, and had always been, about pleasing everyone else. It was the perfect setup for a dysfunctional relationship. While Louise was attracted to Carter because he was charming and seemed "exciting," Carter was attracted to Louise because she never questioned him or held him accountable for his behavior. She would even make excuses for his behavior when her friends would question the way he treated Louise. She knew of his troubled past and of his many failed relationships. Her empathetic heart just went out to him—never questioning if he had a part in the trouble coming his way or in the failed relationships. Of course there were things he did she did not like. He had disappointed her and even left her feeling a little used at times, but she felt she could understand him. She was going to "help him change."

You can see what is coming, can't you? One day someone "better" came along—another woman with more money to enable his irresponsible behavior—and he was gone. Louise was left alone, with less money, lower self-esteem, and was more convinced than ever that she was never meant to find true love or find someone who would truly love and care for her the way she was willing to love and care for another. Of course, this was not true. Nevertheless, the same pattern had been repeated so many times over the last ten years it seemed to be true. What makes this sadder is that had she put in place clear boundaries and expectations, something she had every right to do, it is almost certain she would have had different experiences.

We will talk more about choosing "safe people" in later chapters, but for the time being, allow me to point out that everything about the scenario I just offered as an example should send up a red flag of warning. Sensitivity is great as long as it is purposeful, but too often people take being vulnerable to an unwise extreme. To begin with, not to sound like a cynic, but people who are narcissistic, manipulative, controlling, selfish, and sometimes downright mean, are attracted to these trusting souls like a wolf to a flock of sheep. These "wolves" love people who are "sensitive, give their hearts so freely, and bend over backwards trying to please," but they love them as I love a good rib-eye steak!

Lest you think I am suspicious and untrusting by nature, I actually believe most people are good people or are at least trying to be good people; however, human beings are not perfect and can do and say things that lead to others being hurt. Consequently, a measured approach to opening oneself up to others is wise. If the other person is trustworthy he will show it, and eventually you can love each other with all your hearts. But in the beginning, take it slowly. Have reasonable expectations of the other person's behavior and hold to your expectations. In conclusion, if you're allowing yourself to be extremely vulnerable, giving your heart away to whoever passes by, and are always the person who has to bend over backwards to please everyone, quit that!

Avoidance

Any time people seek to evade the scrutiny of others or avoid personal confrontations with others concerning their feelings or behavior in their relationships, they often place themselves on a slippery slope. Many avoidant people have found themselves in circumstances of deception they never intended because they had gone underground with their feelings. The way it often works is the person feels unappreciated, unloved, not valued, not listened to, mistreated, or otherwise disregarded by another with whom he is in a relationship.

These people often "go along to get along" with others with whom they should be confronting, although it should be noted that confronting some individuals with certain personality disorders or with a history of violence is *not* recommended without a plan and support. In this case, I am referring to the everyday run-of-the-mill type of person who is presumptuous by nature. I speak of the person whom the avoidant person has been enabling to continue to live a selfish life. Whatever the case, for the avoidant person, confronting anyone seems just too hard for her.

Instead, sometimes the avoidant person pretends to be compliant or willing to do something for the other person or for the good of the relationship, but then takes action too late, inadequately, or sabotage the whole thing because of brooding or hostility. This leads to the other person accusing her of being untrustworthy or lying to him—which in a sense she has—but not in the usual way a pathological liar would. Yes, it is still deceptive.

In other instances, anger may build up until they act out. Take Candice for example. Candice has grown weary of her parents—mainly her father—accusing her of being promiscuous and "chasing boys." In reality she has not been doing that at all. If her father, her main critic, would spend time with her or talk to her at other times than when he is accusing her of being "loose," he would likely realize that. At one time she was "Daddy's girl" and enjoyed their relationship. However, now, because evidently he thinks his parental duties are complete or for some other reason, he is pursuing other interests and no longer gives her the love and attention she so desperately wants from her father.

In this case, both Candice and her father are both actually avoidant. Neither of them is willing to express feelings or talk things out. Her father uses other obligations and work to help him avoid and is only voicing his fears, but not taking the time to address his concerns about his daughter in a healthy manner. Finally, Candice's anger builds and a fatalistic mindset sets in, as she begins to wrongly reason that she might as well be doing what her father is accusing her of doing. Initially the attention she gets from boys as she becomes flirtatious makes it seem as if she has made the right choice. Of course, eventually she feels used, but the boys don't listen to her either. She begins to feel that her feelings really aren't that important and becomes even more avoidant about speaking up for herself and her wants and needs. Dad becomes angrier and more convinced he was right about Candice the whole time—refusing to "deal with her anymore!" With that, he leaves the mess he has made to Candice's mother to solve.

These are but a few examples of how people can passively, but intentionally, fail others by avoiding the responsibility to communicate in a healthy way inherent in every relationship. They may cite any number of reasons or excuses for their avoidance. They may vaguely complain to the other person in the relationship or specifically to friends, yet that is not the same as openly expressing their feelings to others with the intent of resolving the issue.

The result: trust gets broken. Others were depending on the avoidant person for help, participation, and compliance, to be dependable, for an expression of love, or another reciprocal gesture, and the avoidant person allowed them to believe they were receiving it. *It's a strange situation when oftentimes the person who was actually being mistreated eventually can become the villain.*

Failing to Do the Important Work in a Relationship

Maintaining a strong and emotionally healthy relationship requires attention to many areas of the bond that exists between the two people. Sometimes people first think of the need to spend time with one another, to speak lovingly to the other, to take time to be romantic, or to do something thoughtful for the other. Better communication is often on the list, but sadly it is usually the most neglected. This can be a costly mistake. People involved in close relationships with others must constantly work through misunderstandings and negative perceptions related to others. Great relationships do not exist because one person is doing everything right. Likewise, relationships do not fall apart because only one person is doing something wrong.

Each must consistently work to clarify the meaning attached to words or actions—especially when the message is not clear and appears hurtful or disrespectful. In his book, *The Science of Trust: Emotional Attunement for Couples,* John Gottman explains how relationships fail. In short, he writes, "Negative events in couple relationships are inevitable . . . If a couple's negative events are not fully processed, then they are remembered and rehearsed repeatedly, turned over and over in each person's mind. Trust begins to erode . . . continually unprocessed negative events . . . involve the erosion of trust, as well as increase . . . the potential for betrayal."

As an example of how this may play out, consider the situation where the revelation of a marital affair from a husband takes his wife totally off guard. She is blindsided because she had recently been on an enjoyable trip with her spouse, or had recently received a thoughtful gift from him, or there had simply been a complete absence of arguing and bickering in the relationship. In spite of all this, the two people had not been communicating and processing the negative events of their lives together. Assumptions were being made about events, words, and feelings. Negative feelings had taken root. Doubt of his wife's love or concern or interest in him had become an accepted truth in his mind and consequently the justifying of his unacceptable behavior began to take place. The fact that he "didn't talk much anymore" did not seem to be a big problem. "Sure, our communication could be better . . ." both would have agreed, but instead of taking action, those "little" problems, unclear messages, and annoyances were ignored a little longer.

Maybe you have heard the old proverbial rhyme, "For Want of a Nail."

For Want of a Nail
For want of a nail the shoe was lost.
For want of a shoe the horse was lost.

> For want of a horse the rider was lost.
> For want of a rider the message was lost.
> For want of a message the battle was lost.
> For want of a battle the kingdom was lost.
> And all for the want of a horseshoe nail.

The point is that small actions, positive or negative, can result in large consequences. If we neglect the small "nails" in our relationships, we run the risk of a catastrophic failure. Yet, making sure that every "nail" is secure can often prevent catastrophe and heartache.

Without a doubt, there are other reasons why trust is broken in relationships. My initial thoughts found here in this chapter are not meant to provide a comprehensive explanation or list of reasons why people can behave in less than a trustworthy manner; rather it was to ease our way into an understanding of an intensely emotional subject. We must not give into the temptation to jump into a discussion about forgiving and trusting others without a little understanding of people in general. People are both predictable and unpredictable and when it comes to trying to solve relationship problems, it is always a good idea to slow down and get as much information or understanding about the other person as well as the events in question, before moving on to trying to address the problem.

Frankly, it can be difficult to make sense of what some people do, or what they are thinking, if the person is not forthcoming with truth and relevant information or truly lacks self-awareness. Sometimes it might just be the unbridled impulsivity of someone with serious impulse control issues. At other times, it can seem that the person lacks a conscience or good common sense. Just the same, I encourage you *not* to label the person or try to diagnose them with some personality disorder. If needed, leave that to a professional.

You trying to do it will accomplish nothing but to drive a wedge between you and that person. No one wants to be in a relationship with a person who thinks he is "sick", "crazy", or mentally broken in some other way. Try first to understand them, to hear them, to learn from and about them. This will not be easy if we're talking about the person who broke your trust or hurt you in some way; nonetheless it may become a major part of *your* healing process. With that said, in chapter two we will move on to the different ways in which trust is often broken.

How Trust is Broken

. . . . . .

The topic of whether or not people are trustworthy can bring out the cynics and the Pollyanna-type optimists alike. Just listen and you are liable to hear some, though not many, in our society insist on the basic good of human beings and try to approach the topic with a reasonableness that borders on the naïve. The majority will probably voice anything from skepticism to seething cynicism about the trustworthiness of people in general. Most have had their opinions influenced or flavored by personal experiences and the attitudes of the people in their family of origin. My goal in this chapter is to present neither perspective. As a result, I will do my best to try to stick with what I know to be the facts. No matter what I think, most will not be persuaded to change their opinions easily and at this point, an open mind is all I ask.

One truth we can all agree on in the beginning is that there are pitfalls, traps, temptations, distractions, human weaknesses, personality disorders, character flaws, dysfunctional families, dysfunctional people, dysfunctional thinking, and so forth to be found in abundance among people in the world in which we live. We can't move too quickly to condemn or to vindicate—as if it were our place to do so in the beginning. Nor can we always neatly explain everything or make sense of it when we have the facts. Some events just leave us scratching our heads.

As John Gottman explains in his book, *The Science of Trust,* primarily, relationships fail over time and a break in trust becomes more likely because of the neglect of the relationship and due to poor communication. He explains first that, "Negative events in couple relationships are inevitable." However, he goes on to explain how the couple's response to these negative events can lead to the failure of the relationship. The following is an abbreviated explanation of the process that leads to failure. "If a couple's negative events are not fully processed, then they are remembered and rehearsed repeatedly, turned over and over in each person's mind. Trust begins to erode [then these] continually unprocessed negative events [result in] the erosion of trust, as well as increase . . . the potential for betrayal." This is where the structural weakening of a relationship takes place. What I will address in the remainder of the chapter are the issues that cause the collapse to take place.

As a counselor I have even found that when someone wants to "spill his guts" about the "whole thing", he or she may not even know how to share everything that is relevant. Sometimes it may take several sessions before I get all the relevant facts. Yes, I know people lie and withhold information. Even so, I have seen individuals be forthcoming with information when I asked for it, only to question innocently, "Is that relevant?" It may have been one of the primary pieces of the puzzle, but he never saw it. Why? Far too many people lack self-awareness and the ability to connect the dots in relational interactions that have taken place over time. Some attribute it to low "emotional intelligence" or low self-awareness.

Two leading researchers on the subject, John D. Mayer and Peter Salovey, explain it this way: "Emotional intelligence refers to an ability to recognize the meanings of emotion and their relationships and to reason and problem-solve on the basis of them. Emotional intelligence is involved in the capacity to perceive emotions, assimilate emotion-related feelings, understand the information of those emotions, and manage them." The same person that can be brilliant and have a high IQ, can lack emotional intelligence and be like a bull in a china shop in their relationships.

Sorry, my optimism slipped out a little, but optimism is not gullibility. My optimism lies more in the idea that if most people aren't full of evil intent, maybe they just need to learn a better way of relating to others. I say all this to build support for not being too quick to demonize people or attribute evil intent to what they do in their relationships. Even when some people mess up and clearly are in the wrong, it doesn't mean it was their intent. Now, let's take a look at how trust is broken in relationships or what causes the collapse.

Indulging an Unhealthy Curiosity Can Lead to Broken Trust

"Attractive nuisances"—pursuing things that are essentially good but that we don't need—I never will forget that was the topic of a speaker at an honor student banquet I attended with my wife when she graduated from college. It's the idea that people will invariably get themselves off track in life or in trouble when they go after things that look good but have little real value. It starts with a lofty goal—not a bad thing—but takes the person in question where he doesn't really *need* to go. An example might be a desire for wealth or possessions that is beyond one's normal means to attain. This might lead to one gambling to come up with more money, losing that money and more, and lying to try to hide it from someone.

Another example might be trying to attain a certain position of power and influence. That's attractive. Still, it becomes a nuisance, a pain in one's life, because of what that person did to attain and maintain that power and influence. Let me give you one more: the desire to feel great instead of under so much pressure and unhappiness. It's a great desire, but when someone starts getting high on drugs to reach that feeling, she will soon find she has welcomed a plague into her life that will drive her to lie, steal, and do other things she never dreamed she would do.

A History of Poor Behavior Can Lead to Broken Trust

Luke was actually hurt that his wife and children acted as if they didn't trust him; it was as if he were an ogre or monster. He could see it. He knew he had a temper, but "everyone gets angry," he would always say in defense of his behavior. But one too many bruises received, one too many fits of anger, one too many nights of trashing the house and sending everyone running for cover like little mice trying to escape a raging lion had left his family apprehensive at best. No, they didn't trust him! Who would? No amount of pleading or promising would change the way his family saw him. He had a history of bad behavior that was more convincing than anything he could say. His only course of action to redeem himself would be to get help, change and write a new history for himself.

Dysfunctional Attempts to Meet One's Needs

The problem in some relational situations where trust is broken is that someone decides the other person in the relationship is not going to meet her emotional or physical needs or does not want to meet her needs, so she goes looking for ways to meet her own needs. This is often the case with people engaging in addictive behavior. They convince themselves that if their needs are going to be met, they will have to meet them. In his must-read book, *Out of the Shadows: Understanding sexual addiction,* Patrick Carnes explains,

The addict's belief system contains certain core beliefs that are faulty or inaccurate and, consequently, that provide a fundamental momentum for the addiction. Generally, addicts do not perceive themselves as worthwhile persons. Nor do they believe that other people would care for them or meet their needs if everything was known about them, including the addiction. Finally, they believe that sex is their most important need. Sex is what makes isolation bearable. Their core beliefs are the anchor points of the sexual addiction. If you do not trust people, one thing that is true about sex—and alcohol, food, gambling, and risk—is that it always does what it promises—for the moment. Thus, as in our definition of addiction, the relationship is with sex—and not people.

In an ironic twist, "the addict knows he is *not* trustworthy" and "in his isolation he is also convinced that most people cannot be trusted." All this leads to a pattern of secretive and deceptive behavior in which the addict continues to break the trust of others, but somehow tells himself that he is justified in whatever he chooses to do. This is but one example of a person engaging in dysfunctional behavior in an attempt to meet his own needs and how a breach in trust can be rationalized as a viable option.

Trusting the Wrong People Can Lead to Broken Trust

Call me what you will, but I don't pet dogs that bite and I don't put trust in people who have never been trustworthy. If they earn the right to be trusted, we can begin, otherwise, they are only reaping what they have sown. Did that sound harsh? Maybe, but far too often I have seen people continue to trust another person who has never, and *I mean never, failed to disappoint* them. "Oh! What am I

going to do?" they cry. "They promised me this time . . ." I just want
to scream, "For the love of Pete, they promise you every time! And
they break their promise every time!" It's like someone trying to pet
a rattlesnake and being utterly amazed the snake bit them. That's
what rattlesnakes do! It's their nature. They're not social reptiles.
Get a bunny. Then if you are bitten, we'll all be amazed with you!

Selfishness Can Lead to Broken Trust

Teens and children are often driven by what they want. It's
actually normal to start out that way. This is why parents have to
teach their children to share with their siblings and playmates, play
nice, consider others, and say "thank you," among other lessons.
With children it's a sign of immaturity, with adults it's a sign of
narcissism and immaturity. But let's get back to children and teens.

Parents are often deeply troubled when their child or teen
disobeys and breaks their trust. It should trouble them. Nevertheless,
it is not always a sign of a troubled child or that the child is going to
grow up to be a criminal. Immature children and teens are usually
impulsive and impressionable—even gullible. This in itself is a setup
for rule breaking for most. They were excited. It was a last minute
thing and they thought it would be okay. They made a judgment call
and it was wrong. If it was something like not keeping a promise, or
lying about doing their homework, or arriving home thirty minutes
late, instead of treating them like a criminal, or labeling them as a
liar, or threatening to send them away to military school, use the
occasion as a teaching moment to connect what they chose with the
consequences. Don't define your child by an occasional mess-up.

That being said, if your child or teen shows a persistent disregard
for rules, others' feelings, laws, or other moral boundaries, it is
possible this behavior is deep-seated and seeking professional

counseling for them and the family would most likely be beneficial. In any case, attempts to teach and model the correct behavior and connecting their choices with the consequences should continue to be taught. I have had parents bring teens to my office for counseling concerning certain behaviors only to find out the parents were doing the same thing. I will never forget the look of confusion on one man's face when I told him that if he wanted his son to stop doing a particular thing he would need to stop doing it as well. This was followed by a look of confusion on my face as to why he didn't get it!

Inappropriate Relationships Can Lead to Broken Trust

In spite of all the "really good reasons" for how they got involved in an inappropriate relationship that have come back to haunt them, some folks just seem to be astonished at their own behavior when they do the same thing again. It's a study all to itself as to why people of all ages get into relationships in which they have no business being involved. Perhaps many situations appear harmless at first—at least to some. Just a few of those avenues are as follows: Internet hookups, social networking, chat rooms, workplace romances, flirting at bars when out without a spouse, or even frequenting strip bars. Even my sixteen-year-old daughter can see the pretense and deception that goes with that territory. Once when she saw a sign advertising a "gentleman's club" she remarked, "Did you ever notice that *real gentlemen* never go to gentlemen's clubs?" Smart girl.

As a marriage counselor, I see a good portion of clients can trace the beginning of their problems back to standard social networks. As you know, social networking sites like *Facebook* are not inherently evil. Sites like this do not endorse or support inappropriate relationships, but it is one more avenue a few people use inappropriately, and quickly they find they have destroyed the trust someone else had in them. It happens when lonely people, many times women, go to social networking sites looking for support and understanding, and along comes what I call "Facebook Fabios." You may remember the popular male model from a few years back named Fabio—muscular, long hair blowing in the breeze—he was on the covers of hundreds of romance novels. A good guy as far as I know.

Nevertheless, these so-called Facebook Fabios seem to troll the waters of Facebook and other similar sites. They seek to appear understanding to women they hear are hurting and feeling distant from their husbands. In fact, "they understand" when that sorry husband won't even talk to them. These Facebook Fabios know just how to soothe the hurting hearts of these women. The problem is obvious in many ways. First, she is married. Second, usually, so is he. Thirdly, if he's not, he's either running with several women, or he has messed up his own life terribly and now is helping someone else do the same, or he lives in his parent's basement and has no real talent for doing much other than causing trouble.

"But we're just friends," some will say. You have other friends less dangerous to your credibility. Louis McBurney advises, "What begins as a pleasant friendship glides silently across the line. The only way to avoid those boundary violations is to watch for the early warning signs. If you begin to notice that someone lights up your life a little too much, back off. If you find yourself looking forward to the next time you can be together, cancel it."

Lying and Deception Can Lead to Broken Trust

Who has lied to you? Someone's name or face possibly came to mind rather quickly. Lies hurt. It is offensive when another lies to you. I will never forget when I was a child that I lied to my dad once. He found out. My rear end hurt for some time. He didn't beat me, he was not abusive. Nevertheless, he made an impression on me. More memorable than his form of discipline was what he said to me. I still remember it some forty years later. "When you lie to me, you're treating me like I'm stupid!" He explained. He went on to talk to me about how disrespectful it was to lie to someone. I never thought my dad was stupid or meant to disrespect him. When I was eighteen, I thought I was smarter than he was—and everyone else—but I never meant to insult him as I apparently had done.

The lie I told as a child was not about attitude or trying to play him for a fool. It was about not getting in trouble. Yes, I had tried to deceive him, but in my childish mind, it was for my own good! I used washcloths to pad my britches once, which helped with the consequences, but it was not always possible to get to the padding before Daddy got to me! Hence, we have the fabrication and distortion of the facts concerning the preceding events of that day—in other words, the lie that got me in trouble.

Not to in anyway justify lying, only to explain one motivation often seen in children, people lie to cover up mistakes, sins, wrongs, deceitful behavior, or just because they are avoidant. Small children, big children, even adults, lie to avoid penalties of some kind. It's a problem common to humans. Neither you nor I will ever be able to eliminate the failing from another human being. Nevertheless, we still cannot allow it to go unchallenged if we know about it. One thing we can do, especially when it pertains to children, is to make it "safe" to tell the truth. In other words, if a child knows they are going to get a "beat down" as one child explained to me, he is probably going to lie. If the child knows Mom or Dad is going to "totally freak out" she will likely tell a lie. You get the picture. The child has to have a reasonable expectation of a calm and rational response that certainly does not involve them being harmed. This will not ensure you will always get the truth the first time, but if you are "safe" to talk to, you have a better chance. We will talk more of this in later chapters. At this point, let us stay on the subject of why and how trust is broken.

Reckless Behavior Can Lead to Broken Trust

People get involved in behavior they should be avoiding. Example: What business does a recovering addict have going to a party where he knows people will be using drugs? That is as crazy as an alcoholic who says she wants to quit drinking hanging out at a bar with her girlfriends, or a man who has been caught cheating on his wife, going to a strip bar! It is likely they're going to mess up and then feel the need to try to lie their way out of it. As my father would have said, "You ain't got no business being there in the first place!" It's not good grammar, but it's true.

Showing Little or No Regard for Those Closest to Us Can Lead to Broken Trust

Sometimes breaking the trust of another is as simple as continually failing to show regard for those closest to us. Often I have heard someone speak of a relationship he has tried to pursue with a loved one or friend only to have that person continually fail to show him any measure of thoughtfulness or show any personal regard for his time or feelings. It's not that she was mean or nasty to him. She was not. In fact, she was neither mean nor nice to him. That was part of the problem. The other person had always treated him as if he were irrelevant. Yet, now due to changes in the life or mindset of the other person, she was interested in having a relationship. In the mind of the person treated as unimportant for years, it was now difficult to connect with the person with whom he had always wanted a relationship. How strange is that? In reality, it's not strange at all. If a person is never emotionally there for the other person, and that has been her history, it is going to be difficult for one to connect with her—even though it was a goal for so long.

It's just part of the human response to draw back from people or relationships where we feel doubt in the other person's intention. We simply don't trust them. Yes, that can change, but the individuals who now want a relationship must understand that they have set the precedent for the way the relationship will go. Now, they have had a change of mind, he or she must earn the right to be trusted by the other person. Similarly, the person who doubts the other's sincerity must take his or her time and warm up to that person over time. Being consistently respected and regarded as important to the other person will feel much more natural and much safer.

I Wish I Knew All the "Whys" And "Hows" Trust Could Be Broken

There are so many reasons why people experience deception, lying, or some other break in the trust they have placed in someone else. In addition to what we have already said, there is the fact that some people have personality traits or in the worst-case scenario, personality disorders that are at the root of their behavior.

Some are so avoidant by nature good communication is difficult. For some, the anxiety or insecurity they feel is so strong it affects their behavior. Others can't stand feeling rejected or are constantly making decisions or saying things just to be accepted by others. Some are extreme introverts in a relationship with strong extroverts and constantly feel overwhelmed by their more vocal and forceful partners and will say whatever they need to just to back them off.

No, none of these justifies deception, lying, or a break in the trust that is supposed to be sacred. However, if we seek to understand people, rather than just demonizing them and their behavior, we can make much more progress in restoring and building healthy relationships. The good news is that, in many cases, if we can get past our hurt we can learn to forgive and rebuild.

Making Sense of It All

The moment we accept we are all flawed human beings, we increase our capacity for understanding and forgiveness. Whether we choose to continue a relationship or whether we have no choice but to continue a relationship, or whether we remain undecided, greater understanding of others and ourselves will remain one of the most beneficial endeavors in which we can invest our time and energy. It is my hope and prayer that by the end of this book you will have more answers and more understanding, but I do not suggest that it will be because of any supposed wisdom I possess that is greater than that of anyone else. My purpose is to lead you and walk with you along this journey as you find your unique answers and understanding that you need to move past the hurt of a broken relationship.

CHAPTER THREE

Forgiveness and Trust

. . . . . .

The unfortunate truth is that the trust that exists between two people can feel as solid and strong as steel one day and lay shattered before them the next. Usually there were smaller breaks or fractures in the relationship leading up to the major break. Maybe those fractures were in the form of feelings of emotional distance, a lack in the sharing of feelings, joys, and even anger. I do not say this to inspire paranoia or suspicion for the other person or to cause one to fear for his or her relationship, only to emphasize all healthy relationships require constant care and awareness of one's needs, weaknesses, and desires as well as those of the other person.

Whether you are relating to a spouse, a child, a friend, or some other type of relationship, to ignore the other person in a relationship by not listening, by not being attentive, or by withholding approval can cause breaks in the relationship bond to form. Furthermore, to fail to actively seek the other's good, to not seek to meet his or her needs, or give him or her your time, and other failing in like measure may cause those fractures to increase or multiply, leading to a shattering of the relationship when under stress. Make no mistake about it; keeping a relationship healthy requires effort. Consider then, how much more effort will it take to rebuild or restore a relationship? Nevertheless, don't lose heart, it can be done.

Allow me to move quickly to the heart of rebuilding trust in a relationship. Rebuilding trust takes time. It will not happen overnight. Thus, we must be committed to the process. Unless you are willing to *consider* forgiveness, for your sake and that of the other person, it is unlikely you will receive much insight from what I have to say. I hope that is not the case. My hope at this point is that you are willing to *consider* forgiving the person who broke your trust. Likewise, for the person who has broken the trust of another, unless you are *willing to consider* asking for forgiveness, you would be wasting your time to pursue the relationship any further.

Restoring relationships ruined through a breach of trust will not be achieved quickly or by people who are half-hearted. Pride has to be put aside. Humility must be present. We must be willing give up the desire for vengeance and address the temptation to throw the misdeed in the face of the other. Mercy must reign in the heart of the person who has been hurt. For the person who caused the injury, there can be no sweeping of wrongs under the rug. A relational balance is required and sometimes it is a struggle to get there.

Forgiveness Is Essential

Since you are still reading you must have signed on for what is ahead. So, let us begin. *It is important to understand that just because we are beginning with a conversation about forgiveness does not mean that forgiveness must or will take place first.* I have begun here because I have had numerous couples come in for marriage counseling due to an affair or due to one of the two having a drug or gambling problem as if they were trying to save the marriage, when in reality they were only checking things off their list on the way to the lawyer's office.

In those cases, one of them had already made up his or her mind that the marriage was over.

Likewise, I have had a few parents bring their troubled teen in for me to "fix", only to find out later that they had already decided to pass him on to another parent, or in some way, put out of the house. In all of these cases the people had most likely waited too late to really be objective about getting help. Too much had been said or done, or not said or done and they just wanted to say they had tried everything before they gave up. Had they sought professional help sooner maybe things could have been different. I don't know. What I do know is that it might have been possible to find forgiveness down the road if they had been open to continuing the struggle a bit longer. In some cases, years later, they will learn to forgive. In other cases, they will live the remainder of their lives alienated and bitter. I have seen both happen.

My only purpose in sharing this is to emphasize just how important it is to be willing to consider forgiving. Just being willing to consider forgiving makes it possible to begin the journey. Forgiveness is an essential part of rebuilding trust in a relationship because it is the willingness to offer forgiveness, in some measure, to the one who has wronged another that opens the door for the rebuilding process to begin. The problem is that forgiveness is not always easy and it does not fully take place at one point in time. There may be a point at which we say, "Today, I realized I have forgiven them." Even though there was a point and time at which we realize forgiveness has taken place, there was a period of time leading up to that during which we struggled with the idea or the process of reconciling the events of the past.

I have seen people who immediately proclaim their forgiveness for the person who has wronged them, then struggle with maintaining their forgiving attitude. There are others who steadfastly hold to the fact they have been wronged and state they may never be able to forgive or that they simply cannot forgive the other person. What is interesting is that, whatever the initial feeling, the person's feelings often change back and forth over time until the issue is resolved.

The way it sometimes plays out is that the person who was quick to "forgive" finds the more they think about it the more they realize they have not yet forgiven. Likewise, the person who *could not* forgive eventually finds it in his or her heart to forgive—if for no other reason than for his or her own good. For this reason, one of the first steps a couple should take after the trust in a relationship has been broken is to slow things down. There are no simplistic answers and no quick fixes—but there is hope.

Trust Is Essential

Betrayal creates a crisis and ignites a flood of emotions and gives life to a whole new set of fears. Whether it is a marital affair, the unexpected arrest of a spouse or child, finding out one is financially ruined because another gambled away all the money, or you've been stabbed in the back by the words or actions of a dear friend or family member, rebuilding trust with that individual is not going to be easy. If the relationship survives, you and that person have work to do. Just as rebuilding a relationship requires the work of forgiveness, it also requires work to rebuild the trust. The reason I emphasize this is to address the erroneous idea that the gratitude felt by the forgiven person should motivate that person to become instantly trustworthy. It can happen, it could happen, but it doesn't always happen. It takes time to live out or demonstrate a change of heart. Sometimes it takes time for the change of heart to affect the person's whole being—words, thoughts, and actions.

Additionally there is the idea, spoken or unspoken, that because one has received forgiveness, now the past is the past and he will never be questioned again. The way it often plays out is that when the person who offered forgiveness questions something the forgiven person does, has done, or was supposed to have done, the forgiven person explodes and says something like, "I thought you forgave me. Why are you treating me this way? I said I was sorry! You said you forgave me! Why won't you just let it go?"

There is a penalty to breaking someone's trust and grace may take away the judgment, but it won't take away the sting. Slow down. Take the time to rebuild the trust. Do it for the other person in your relationship as well as for the relationship itself. Do it for yourself. In the process of rebuilding the trust, you will develop greater understanding for one another while rebuilding your credibility. Rebuilding the trust will make the forgiveness sweeter and the relationship stronger.

Unity of Purpose Is Essential

Some of the best advice on the subject of forgiveness I have ever read came from Dr. Lewis Smedes. He has written numerous books, any of which I would recommend, but for now I would like to share some brief excerpts of his wisdom. Particularly relevant to work of rebuilding trust in a relationship is his statement that, "It takes one person to forgive; it takes two people to be reunited." This strikes a note with me because I often see couples who can't seem to get together on the rebuilding process. The repentant person is willing to "do anything," while at the same time the person who was wronged is often unwilling to let the other person off that easily and allow sufficient penance to be done. Eventually, the person who felt wronged will become cooperative and begin to show a forgiving attitude, but depending on the other person's personality, and how long she has been dangled over the fire, she may respond by declaring she is "tired of trying."

This brings us to an important point in the early stages of repairing a relationship. It's the point at which there has to be a conscious decision to work together on the problem at the same time. I often draw the comparison between a couple's behavior to that of a person playing with the children's game called a Chinese finger puzzle or as some call it, a Chinese handcuffs. The "puzzle" or "handcuffs" is really just a cylindrical tube, often made of thin woven strips of bamboo. The player can easily insert the index finger of each hand into the opposite ends of the puzzle. However, when the player tries to pull his fingers out of the tube at the same time, the tube or puzzle tightens onto the fingers, "trapping" the person. It appears the person is handcuffed. The secret to getting free is to push both fingers inward at the same time, releasing the pressure, and then remove one's fingers one at a time.

My point is this: The "finger puzzle" represents the problem of broken trust. Both people in the relationship are attached to the problem through their spoken desire to save the relationship. It is natural that both will initially not display the same intensity when working on the problem. In other words, there will be varying degrees of participation at first and this can cause a problem that must be resolved. For example, during the process of restoring the trust and achieving true forgiveness, when one person in the relationship pulls away from the other, even though the other person is moving toward him, the first person's retreat leaves him bound and unable to accomplish the desired goal of rebuilding the relationship. When the response is reversed, the same thing happens, just with opposite results. When both withdraw from the other at the same time, both will become more tightly bound by the problem than ever before.

The only solution that will free them both in this process is for each to move toward the other at the same time. When this is done, each will usually begin to feel released from the problem and emotionally drawn toward the other person. This, in turn, is the beginning of the relationship being freed from what has bound it.

One reason it appears to work this way is that when we see another moving toward us relationally in good faith, it is easier to trust him than it is when we feel he is moving away from us. Often when a person withdraws or moves away, the immediate feeling is often a sense of rejection. In some cases, it appears suspicious and we may wonder what the other person is trying to hide or if the other person is trying to control or manipulate us. Either way, trust crumbles and uncertainty once again has control. Later we will talk more about what it means to "move toward" the other person, but for now, it suffices to say that two people must work in unison on restoring trust to give the relationship its best chance for survival.

Forgiveness and Trust Are Bound Together

Which comes first, forgiveness or trust? I can't say. It depends on so many variables and the people involved. For some, they can't forgive until they can trust. For others, they can't trust until they have forgiven. Rather than saying it is one before the other, let us agree that it is a commitment to work on both at the same time. One will likely be resolved before the other, but why box ourselves in and say it has to be one way or the other. We know both have to take place, so let us begin with both as our goal.

Although we will discuss numerous types of trust violations, let's consider one of the most often cited reasons for being unable to trust another person—the extramarital affair. Few transgressions come close to the hurt brought by an extramarital affair. It violates the most sacred of relationships and devastates a person's capacity to feel at ease with the spouse that broke the vow. Furthermore, not all will be mended with a simple exchange of, "I'm sorry" and an "I forgive you." Without restoring the trust there will be little to support the relationship. Remorse and absolution may provide a beautiful moment, but failing to restore the trust to the relationship will undermine all that has been gained.

In his book, *Forgiving the devil: Healing damaged relationships,* Dr. Terry D. Hargrave makes the point that,

The heart of forgiveness and restoration is not so much about letting go of the transgression of the affair, as it is restoring as much love and trust to the relationship as possible. If a victimized spouse simply lets go of the transgression of an affair and forgives, and the victimizing spouse has one extramarital relationship after another, then the forgiveness has accomplished little. Forgiving untrustworthy behavior is not forgiveness, but fool heartiness [sic]. Forgiveness has to be about restoring trust and it most often happens a little at a time, over a long period of time.

Obviously, without a commitment to offering forgiveness and rebuilding the trust in the relationship at the same time, the foundation of that relationship will not be a stable one. I realize it is difficult when two people in a relationship have known a relationship built on trust. Being placed in the position of having to forgive a betrayal and then rebuild the trust in a relationship that has known trust—but lost it—is a crushing blow. It would be similar to being told the house you have almost finished building has to be completely dismantled and rebuilt because the foundation was faulty and is not up to building codes, and the only way it can be fixed is to start over.

The enormity of it all sets in and the first reaction may be despair, frustration, hopelessness, or feeling as if one does not have enough strength to start over again. However, the good news is that, as with the house that has to be rebuilt, it is possible. There is a plan. There are tools and resources. It can be done! The biggest struggle might just be making one's mind up that one is going to do it. The dream was almost a reality. It can still be a reality. We take a deep breath and we start over. This is where we begin when we find ourselves with shattered dreams. It's a starting place—it's no place to live the rest of one's life.

If you're unsure of whether you want to rebuild the relationship or not, that's okay, you will still benefit from the discussion of forgiveness in the next chapter. If you feel your relational destination is to rebuild the relationship, then with that in sight let us begin our journey. Just keep in mind, it takes time and it may not be easy, but it is possible. It can be done.

CHAPTER FOUR

The Nature of Forgiveness

· · · · · ·

When we look at the various aspects of working out one's thoughts and feelings of forgiveness, the scope of the effort is amazing. It makes the gift of being forgiven by another even more humbling and highlights the graciousness of the one who offers forgiveness. Forgiveness has a grace about it, but it is also deliberately powerful in its work—setting both the offender and the offended free. We are well acquainted with how the offender is set free, but what about the offended? Lance Morrow highlights a measure of the power of forgiveness for the offended when he writes, Not to forgive is to be imprisoned by the past, by old grievances that do not permit life to proceed with new business. Not to forgive is to yield oneself to another's control . . . to be locked into a sequence of act and response, of outrage and revenge, tit for tat, escalating always. The present is endlessly overwhelmed and devoured by the past. Forgiveness frees the forgiver. It extracts the forgiver from someone else's nightmare.

Do you want to know real freedom? Do you want to experience relief from the burden you have felt over the wrong done to you? Are you weary of feeling violated or dishonored by someone's deception? You will never be able to change the past. You will never be able to control the other person—all attempts are fantasy. You can only control yourself and what you think and what you do. You have that choice. It wasn't your choice to be deceived or let down. Nevertheless, it is your choice as to what you will do with what has happened. Forgive and be free. Don't forgive and be controlled by another's actions.

Making Sense of What It Means to Forgive

You and I will experience less frustration, and so will the person you are trying to forgive, if you and I can define, in some manner, *what the ability to forgive means to you and what you and I need to be able to be at peace with forgiveness.* This can be a struggle. You may find yourself wrestling with ideas and feelings that are difficult to reconcile. This is because it is difficult for anyone who has been deeply hurt to reconcile the facts, feelings, and thoughts about the past and the thoughts about the future as well as the meaning of all that has taken place. Forgiving can be messy and is not the exact science some would like to make it.

Trying to forgive as someone else thinks you should, or as the other person would, may not work for you. Such was the case with Jane. In the face of a checkered past and a series of broken promises, Jane had told her husband Neal that she would forgive him of the verbal abuse she had suffered as the result of his inability or unwillingness to control his temper. He had never physically harmed her, but had left her emotionally black-and-blue as the result of one of his recent tirades. He had promised he wouldn't do it again countless times, but this time he had made good on his promise for several weeks, only to fall back in his old ways.

What hurt her more this time was that he had done better just long enough for her to believe he was changing. She had gotten her hopes up only to be disappointed once again. As you might expect, Neal cited the fact that he had "been doing better" lately as the basis of why she should forgive him.

"Why can't you just let it be?" Neal pleaded. "What do you want from me?" This was his way of implying she was being unreasonable.

For him it was simple. He said he was sorry, now let's forget and go out and have a good time. Little did he know that his question of, "What do you want from me?" was the key for Jane.

Jane could forgive Neal in the sense of pardoning him or not trying to punish him for his behavior. She knew he had anger problems when she married him and had forgiven him many times. Now things were different. Forgiving had come to mean something different. It no longer meant overlooking his behavior as it was in the beginning. She could pretend it or dismiss it as just being the way he was, or turn her feelings on and off like a switch. Worn down by years of hurtful words, forgiving was more of a two-person deal than ever before. Now, forgiving could only take place if the inflicting of wounds ceased. She felt conflicted; she knew she had to forgive for her own good, and until now, she had been able to move on, but not now. She knew in her heart even if she genuinely forgave him again the relationship could not be restored—not to what she needed— unless Neal really changed. She could love him benignly from this point on, but she would have to do it for her own sake; it could no longer be to try to make the relationship okay, because it was not and would never be as long as forgiveness only meant, "let's start over."

Jane could love Neal. She could choose not to punish him for his past deeds. She could choose not to bring the past up in their arguments. She even felt she could stay married to him. The one thing she couldn't do at this point was trust Neal not to hurt her again, and that would prevent the relationship from being all it could become. At the moment, there was no confidence in Jane's mind that Neal would be able or willing to nurture her emotionally. She could go just so far in reconnecting with him until he learned to respect her boundaries concerning his behavior. It was not okay for him to treat her any way he chose. Since Jane had suffered because of Neal's behavior and choices, she had a right to say, "It's not okay for you to treat me that way," and she had a right to hold him to a different standard than she had in the past—if the relationship were to continue.

At this point the person who is trying to forgive, is often accused by the offender of not truly forgiving him, or of trying to "control" him. Usually, when a person has suffered numerous wrongs in a relationship he or she is usually what we call "codependent." A simple definition of a codependent person is that the person sees the relationship she is in as being more important than she is. It almost sounds like a sacrificial, noble type of love, but it is not. It is just one-sided. One always demands and the other accommodates. "No" is not an acceptable response. For that matter, "wait" or "maybe" is also viewed as unacceptable. The codependent person, therefore, "goes along to get along," pacifies, caves in, or enables the other person to do as he or she pleases without regard for the codependent person. Any time the codependent person attempts to hold the other person accountable, the offender, Neal in our story, reacts badly to get the codependent person, Jane, to surrender.

NOTE: One of the biggest weapons used against people attempting to employ boundaries is guilt. When Neal exploded with, "Why can't you just let it be?" and "What do you want from me?" he was attempting to use guilt to get Jane to submit to his wishes. This is important: for a codependent person who is not accustomed to setting boundaries, guilt eats away at her boundaries like an acid eats away at metal. Guilt is corrosive and when not addressed properly will eventually destroy all boundaries previously set up. Does this sound like you? Do you often feel guilty? Do you sometimes not even know why you feel guilty? If your answer is yes, watch for guilt to be used against you to get you to give in to other's wishes. A professional counselor can help you explore this and learn a new way of thinking.

For now let's go back to Jane and Neal for one last observation. The offender (Neal) wants *everything* to be all right. He does not want his actions or words to haunt him or his relationship in any way. They are stuck to some degree. Neal has gone too far too many times. Jane has had it! Still she is torn. She feels guilty at the thought of leaving and is uncertain about wanting to stay. She doesn't want forgiveness to mean Neal gets another pass on his behavior. Neal could move the relationship in a positive direction quickly if he would respect her boundaries and mend his ways. Unfortunately, at this point, he is not ready for that. Although he accuses her of trying to control him, ironically he is trying to control her! For now, he will stick to what has always worked, wearing Jane down with guilt and talk of her being unreasonable and unfair until she caves. But such is the uneasy peace that is often the result of someone's being deeply hurt by breaking her trust by another. Perhaps, Neal will earn Jane's trust in the future by truly changing and Jane will find the man who hurt her has the ability to be the man who helps her heal. Only time will tell.

Forgiveness Benefits the Forgiver

When a breach of trust has taken place, the idea many often have is that forgiveness is *necessary* for the relationship, or it is the *right thing to do.* Friends and family, and even some who would offer counsel, will often try to persuade the person who has been hurt to forgive for a number of essentially good reasons such as:

- for "the sake of your marriage" (or future marriage)
- for the "kids"
- to preserve the friendship
- because "they're your child"
- "They didn't mean it . . ."
- because "the Bible tells us to" and it's the "Christian thing to do"
- And countless other sentiments

As noble as this may sound to others, it can sound offensive to the person who has been deceived. The whole idea that the person who was hurt now has to take the high road, do the right thing, or further be the responsible one because of what someone who was trusted has done only seems to add insult to injury. The feelings expressed usually go something like this, "I see how it is, I was the one done wrong and now you want me to be the one to make everything okay by forgiving! If you say you're sorry and I don't forgive you then I become the bad guy. That's not fair!"

Truly, the person hurt by a breach of trust is in an unfair position. The very fact that the other person disrespected him through deception is not right. Now, for it to sound as if the one who broke his trust and those around him just want him to forgive the person so that the problem will go away, it can hardly feel anything but offensive and unfair. Granted, others involved usually don't have such an extreme or simplistic point of view, yet it can feel very much like that is reality to a hurting person.

The Benefits of Forgiving

Not to promote what some might see as a selfish mentality, but I would suggest a starting point for the person who has been hurt might be to consider the truth, that in many ways, forgiveness will benefit her far greater than the person being forgiven. Accordingly, one should primarily forgive for her own sake. Yes, that may sound selfish, but it is honest and it is best. The reality of being human is that people rarely do anything that does not benefit them. This is no time to be a martyr, or conversely, to play the role of a person who is above being hurt deeply. You don't have to tell anyone you are forgiving first for your own well-being, nevertheless, if you don't start with your own welfare, your commitment to follow through on forgiving could be short-lived. It could even die altogether the moment the person who broke your trust speaks or behaves in an insensitive way toward your feelings.

Allow me to give you a few more reasons to begin to forgive for your own good. First, do it for your health. In an article by the Mayo Clinic on *Forgiveness: Letting go of bitterness and grudges*, a number of benefits are highlighted for the one who forgives. According to the article,

"Letting go of grudges and bitterness can make way for compassion, kindness and peace. Forgiveness can lead to:

- Healthier relationships
- Greater spiritual and psychological well-being
- Less anxiety, stress, and hostility
- Lower blood pressure
- Fewer symptoms of depression
- Lower risk of alcohol and substance abuse

The reality of holding a grudge, or unforgiveness in one's heart, can be compared to carrying around toxic waste in one's pockets— eventually it will poison the person or worse. What's more, until the person carrying the unforgiveness sees the benefits of getting rid of it, there's not much anyone can do to help her. No matter how much others try to convince us to forgive, until we see there is something in it for us, it's likely we won't even try. That being said, it doesn't have to be the same for everyone. Nevertheless, everyone must find a reason that will truly motivate him or her since *just* the guilty person's apology alone will probably not provide a great deal of motivation.

Various motivations that help some people get started on the road to forgiveness are:

- One's emotional or physical health
- One's religious beliefs
- Because one truly loves the other person
- Because the person has failed in a similar way
- For the sake of preserving the family unit
- For the sake of preserving the marriage
- And many other reasons

This is not to say that any of these reasons or other reasons will make forgiving easy. I don't know of anything that makes a deep hurt *easy* to forgive. I am only trying to help us get started on the journey. The alternative to not beginning the journey is to remain stuck in the hurt like a man in quicksand. If one remains stuck in unforgiveness, like the quicksand, it will slowly engulf the person until it has swallowed him or her up. You can know if that has happened to someone, or to oneself, because the person will be consumed by bitterness.

Forgiveness Can Take Time

When people say things like, "Well, you just need to forgive and move on." they are usually just tired of hearing us talk about the event or have no other answer or suggestion to give. This is why *others will usually be ready for us to forgive before we are ready to forgive.* As much as we might want unforgiving people to put us, and them out of the misery of having to tell or hear the story of hurt again, we can't push them.

In the event you are that person and you're even making yourself miserable talking about the past, don't push yourself to forgive or allow others to push you to forgive. It won't help. Sometimes simply talking repeatedly about the hurt or disappointment causes us to feel pressured. It also might be a sign you may be living your life around the centerpiece of your hurt and disappointment. In other words, everything seems to be connected or revolve around or lead back to the hurt and disappointment. If this is the case, allow me to suggest a few ideas:

- Limit the amount of time you spend talking about it.
- Don't constantly talk to the same person about it.
- Don't allow yourself to rehearse the events in your mind over and over.
- When you find yourself dwelling on the events, stop what you're doing and engage yourself in a new task to break that train of thought.
- Listen to soothing music or a relaxation recording when trying to go to sleep so that you don't spend that time ruminating on the past events.
- Give permission to a trusted friend or family member to hold you accountable to your pledge of no longer constantly talking about it.
- When/if you pray don't just review the hurtful events; spend time in thanksgiving and seeking for a purpose in which you can invest yourself.
- See a professional counselor who can help you find ways to move forward.

As the old saying goes, "Rome wasn't built in a day," likewise any meaningful life changes will take time.

Forgiveness Can Be Complicated

German classical scholar and philosopher Friedrich Nietzsche stated succinctly, "I'm not upset that you lied to me, I'm upset that from now on I can't believe you." When trust is broken in a relationship, something is lost. Suddenly, something of great importance is just gone and "sorry" just doesn't fix it. Even when all involved want it to be okay—it's just not okay. At this point *it is good and often necessary* even for the most forgiving person to say, "I love you and I will forgive you, but it's not okay."

Let's consider those last three statements: I love you. I forgive you. But it's not okay. As they say on Sesame Street, "Which of these three don't belong?" Actually they all belong together, but the last statement doesn't seem to fit. In fact, one will find many who do not like it being tagged on to the end. They want to hear, "I love you and I forgive you." But it's not okay. "If you love me and you forgive me it has to be okay!" Doesn't it? No. It does not.

The reason I venture down this road of clarification is that sometimes when a person who has been wronged feels that, if she forgives the person who wronged her, she will have to accept what has been done to her as just "one of those things" that happens in life. Perhaps she may feel she would need to respond or behave as if it were "no big deal." The offended person does not want to minimize the wrong and should not be placed in that position. (We will talk more about minimizing later). The freedom to say to the offender, "It's not okay," after responding, "I love you and I forgive you", gives the offended person the necessary sense of validation she needs.

It's her way of rightfully saying she is justified in feeling hurt. It is reasonable for her to feel the way she does. It wasn't *her* misunderstanding. It wasn't *her* fault. She wasn't easily offended. She has the right to feel wronged. The person who hurt her *cannot and should not* try to take that from her. To do so would be the equivalent of saying she had no right to be offended or it was an insignificant offense. When the person causing the offense, apologizes and essentially desires a response of, "I love you and I forgive you" but doesn't want the "It's not okay" portion, it's because he feels guilty and wants the person who has been hurt to relieve him of the guilt he feels by saying, "It is okay." Don't do it. It is okay for him to feel guilty for a while—*refrain from helping him with that feeling*—because it shows his conscience is at work. In the New Testament, we read that, "For the kind of sorrow God wants us to experience leads us away from sin and results in salvation. There's no regret for that kind of sorrow" (2 Corinthians 7:10 NLT).

Yes, even God wants us to experience sorrow when we do wrong that we might be turned in the right direction. Furthermore, this sorrow or regret needs to run its course so the lesson is learned and an impression is made on the heart and mind of the person who did the wrong. It is okay for people who do wrong to feel badly about it. That is the way God made us. The key is to allow them to feel guilty for doing wrong, not to try to make them feel guilty by harassing them with their mistakes. Simply refrain from consoling them. Just let them think about what they did for a while.

Forgiveness Can Only Do So Much

Forgiveness can seem magical when spoken of by some. It can feel wonderful. It can bring greatly longed-for healing. It can do many splendid things, but can't always make everything right or acceptable in some situations. The one inescapable truth is that no matter how one feels about forgiveness or what stands to be accomplished by giving forgiveness, it all begins with an intellectual decision to offer forgiveness. I say "intellectual" because feelings cannot be allowed to dictate the process beginning or being completed. It must begin as an act of the will. This requires some determination to logically walk oneself through a rational scrutiny of the process and of the feelings one is sure to encounter. There are numerous ways to approach this. We will talk about a few.

Let us begin with forgiveness within the context of a marriage relationship that has been broken through infidelity. In his book, *The Art of Falling in Love*, author and internationally known speaker, Joe Beam, says forgiveness is a set of three decisions.

> First, decide to view the other person as a flawed human being rather than evil personified. When you put another into that category, you do not continue to vilify them because you realize that you, too, are flawed . . . By granting them the right to be a human, however flawed, you can find the ability to make the second decision.
>
> Second, decide that you will not take vengeance, even if that is your right . . . I define vengeance as trying to make the other person hurt as badly as you hurt. That never works.
>
> Third—and this step is optional—restore or develop a relationship with the person who hurt you. This is where forgiving becomes more divine than human . . . In those relationships, there may well be a better future for each of us if I do make the third step and decide to restore the relationship.

Note that he says restoring the relationship is optional. In some situations, even though we may acknowledge we are all flawed human beings, refrain from vilifying them, not seek vengeance, and forgive them, it does not mean that such relationships can or should be restored. Forgiveness can do many wonderful things, but it has limitations in the area of human relationships. In no way am I implying we shouldn't try to restore the relationship—especially when it comes to marriages—but I have seen cases when decisions had been made and circumstances were such that even forgiveness couldn't fix things. My point is only that a person can go too far and no matter how much he or she accuses the other person of "not letting it go" or "not truly forgiving", the fact remains, he/she went too far and now they must reap what they have sown. (See Galatians 6:7)

The Limited Ability of Forgiveness

Now, consider the limited ability of forgiveness in relationships with others in a family situation. Take a moment to reflect on the story of Rodney, a well-meaning teen with no real desire to hurt anyone, but who also lacks good judgment, as do many teens. Rodney likes to smoke weed or pot (marijuana). He argues it doesn't hurt anyone and it doesn't hurt him. Rodney's parents know about his pot use, but they did the same thing when they were his age and feel that if they "give him his freedom," a mutual trust and respect will be observed in the relationship. Their only boundary was that he stay away from "that guy down the street" who they know sells marijuana and a little of everything else. They felt the guy was "bad news."

Rodney had always observed that boundary until one evening he and his friends were going out and they were out of "weed." Just down the street there was a ready supply. What would it hurt this one time? In his teenage wisdom he decides to make an exception just this one time and quickly stops and buys some pot. The dealer, thinking it would be funny, decided to give Rodney something a little "extra." Unknown to Rodney, the pot already rolled into joints, was "laced" with cocaine.

Rodney didn't realize it at the time, but he got a little more than he expected. As the evening went on and he and his friends made their different stops meeting up with their friends, his behavior and driving became more erratic. Sometime after eleven that night Rodney and his friends were in a terrible accident. The person in the other car was killed and Rodney's parents arrived at the police station to find their son behind bars. He was sorry for breaking his parents' trust, but being sorry didn't help. His parents were sorry for taking such a casual attitude about his drug use, but that didn't help either.

In this instance, in theory, forgiveness could be given, trust could be rebuilt. Responsible behavior could become the priority and the standard. However, none of that could rectify the situation.

The harsh realities concerning the limits of forgiveness should serve as a word of warning for any who would take their potentially harmful actions and words lightly. Some have joked, "It's easier to get forgiveness than permission" when trying to bypass someone who would question his/her behavior. My response would be, "Maybe, but even forgiveness cannot erase the consequences set in motion by what was said or done." In the following chapter we will take a moment to consider the nature of trust.

CHAPTER FIVE

The Nature of Trust

. . . . . .

Trusting people can *seem* like a gamble at times, so much so that I have known people who have stated all they needed was their pet to be loved and happy. They were finished with people. "Animals you can trust," I heard someone say. She went on to explain that animals, or pets in this case, are always loyal and loving and are happy to see you every time you come home. I understand the sentiment. Likewise, I have known people who were surrounded by people that should be eyed with suspicion. Many live and work among some extremely dysfunctional people. However, to some degree, we choose to trust someone in some way every day—if only by hoping they will come through for us.

Sharon and Nancy sat talking at lunch about the times in their lives when they realize they had been deceived.

"Trusting people is a game for fools," Nancy observed.

"Well . . . I don't know," Sharon began as if she were trying to come up with a logical reason for Nancy's not being right. "Some people are trustworthy," she continued.

"Who? Your mom?" Nancy questioned with a laugh.

Sharon got quiet and looking down slightly and then out the window of the restaurant, she bit her bottom lip.

Immediately Nancy's eyes widened and she gasped, "You didn't!" She was so loud that even some of the other patrons turned and looked her way. Lowering her head and her voice, she leaned toward Sharon and yelled in a whisper. "You didn't! Tell me you didn't take him back!"

Sharon looked back at Nancy with a pitiful and somewhat embarrassed look on her face, "Well . . . he said he was sorry. You should have been there. He said he had changed. He had learned from his mistakes. He was so sweet," she said, now looking more wistful and hopeful.

"After all he put you through . . . the man is a parasite and a pathological liar! Just when you were getting back on your feet . . . I can't believe it," Nancy paused shaking her head in disbelief. "You never learn," as if knowing she had lost the battle.

Nancy had her right to feel as though she did because of all Sharon's ex-husband Ken had put her through—years of broken promises and of bleeding Sharon dry of resources and emotional strength. Nancy thought when the divorce was final Ken was gone for good. On top of that, Nancy wondered if Sharon had forgotten all those months of crying, sadness, and anger she had spent working through the pain and working Ken out of her system. It didn't make sense.

Such is much of the human experience in relationships. So much doesn't make sense when examined in light of the facts. As with love, forgiveness, caring, and other aspects of human relationships, it is not unheard of for us to find ourselves in a situation where interaction on this level with others can feel uncertain. It is possible to not trust other people, just as it is possible not to love others, or care for them, or forgive them, but consider what you stand to lose and the person you are likely to become if you follow that path. *I would rather be disappointed for believing in someone than to have the character of a person who doesn't believe in anyone.*

Trust Is a Human Need

Either by choice or by necessity, we need to be able to trust. Boundaries help keep us safe. Wisdom helps in our decisions, but the risk must be taken. R.C. Mayer offered some clarification on the nature of trust in an article on the subject of organizational trust. His expanded definition was that, "Trust is defined as a person's (the trustor) willingness to be vulnerable to another person (the trustee) on the basis that the trustee will act according to the trustor's confident expectations." I like this definition because it goes further than only explaining it as "reliance" or "confidence" and the like. Note that he said trust is the "willingness to be vulnerable to another person." It is to lay down our defenses and put ourselves at risk. And we *need* to do this? What is wrong with us? Nothing. Not a thing.

The problem is not with the act of trusting others or being vulnerable. It is the way we develop lasting, deep, meaningful relationships that will enrich our lives. The problem is that we are sometimes careless or unwise in extending our trust. We do not always communicate well our expectations to others. We can expect too much. We can demand too much. We can expect too little. We can give too little. We can get sloppy in our relationships or not tend to them as we should. We can even allow the wrong people into our lives. A different approach to trusting others is what we often need, not to abandon all hope of being able to trust others.

Trust Can Be Risky

There's no way I'm going to deny it—trusting others can be risky. Most would respond, "Well, of course, that's just part of life." I'm talking specifically to people who have been burned. These are the people who took the risk and it didn't turn out well. Tell that person, "Trusting others can be risky," and they will respond, "Yes, and that's why I'm not going to do it again!"

Writing on "Trust," Carolyn McLeod, offers this note on the reality of trusting others,

> Trust is important, but it is also dangerous. It is important because it allows us to form relationships with others and to depend on others—for love, for advice, for help with our plumbing, or what have you—especially when we know that no outside force compels them to give us such things. But trust also involves the risk that people we trust will not pull through for us; for, if there were some guarantee that they *would* pull through, then we would have no need to trust them. Thus, trust is also dangerous. What we risk while trusting is the loss of the things that we entrust to others, including our self-respect, perhaps, which can be shattered by the betrayal of our trust.

How do we minimize the risk? We have to ask ourselves if placing trust in the person in question is ultimately necessary. Some have an intense feeling they "have to have someone" or at least need someone in their lives. This can be the case with teens and some people who have been single for a long time. Some people just can't seem to be happy without that special someone in their lives. This doesn't mean something is wrong with them; it does mean they must exercise their best judgment. This is one reason I recommend the book, *Safe People*, by authors Cloud and Townsend, to everyone, *especially* to anyone who is looking to start a relationship with someone new. We need to know how to find people who will offer a safer relationship and we need to know how to offer someone else a safe relationship.

We can also be wise about the circumstances in which we trust another. Is the situation ripe for deception? Someone offers to invest money for you, but his qualifications are in doubt, he offers no documentation and no way for you to check on your investment. *He* will keep you posted. Something smells fishy.

Perhaps your spouse has a problem of being a compulsive shopper and has run up some hefty credit card bills in the past. Should you not question the multiple credit cards you see in his wallet? Should you not check your credit report? Of course you should. Having no boundaries or not having a means of accountability concerning the possibility of overspending would not be wise. Yet people are often shocked to find their spouses have, or almost have, thrown them into bankruptcy by hiding their compulsive spending practices. To make matters worse, their spouses often knew they had a problem but just didn't want to address it. All the screaming and calling one's spouse a liar and accusing him of being deceptive won't change the fact that both allowed a situation to develop that was ripe for a breach of trust.

Minimize the Risk So Trust Can Grow

The idea of putting into practice personal accountability and boundaries will work in all types of situations to help prevent a violation of the trust in a relationship. However, remember the goal is to establish accountability and boundaries—not control—to minimize a breach of trust, and still this will not guarantee it. When we are talking about people and relationships, the hope of control is an illusion. Furthermore, no matter how much control one exercises over another, it can never be enough to ensure genuine trust. If nothing else, the person seeking to control another will only feel the need to control grow over time to reduce his or her anxiety about the relationship. Eventually the idea of giving up any perceived control will only increase the fear one has that if the person is released from his or her control, that person will surely fail in some way. Controlling another person is never the path to trust.

Examples of relational situations with which people struggle could be: knowing who your children and teens are with, where they are, what they are doing at all times if possible. You don't have to be with them to safeguard their behavior, but you do need to know what is going on in their lives. Likewise, spouses should be accountable to their partners at all times. As a rule, married people have no business doing whatever, whenever, and being with whomever they wish without their spouses knowing about it. (We will talk more of this in later chapters) When we marry we are choosing to be accountable, to honor, to consider, and to live our lives in a way that is beneficial to both.

"But if you trust them why do you need to do that?" some might ask. People are not perfect, that is why we need boundaries and accountability. With many people boundaries and accountability help them to feel secure, cared about, connected to another. In addition, people do not always see the potential for danger or harm because of a limited perspective or personal bias. We can be an objective voice for our family or spouses or friends. No, they will not always appreciate it or think we are right. We might not always be right. Do it anyway. You will do more good than harm by staying involved in the life of the person you love.

Two good examples are my parents and my wife. In my later teen years my parents were dumb as a bag of rocks. By the time I reached my thirties they had become smart people. Either raising me helped make them smarter or they were smart or wise the whole time. I think it was the latter. I thank God and them for the boundaries and accountability they demanded. It worked! I will never forget a boy at school one day saying in a boastful way, "My old man don't care what I do." If that were true, how sad was his situation? I remember being offended he called his father, "my old man" and thinking, *Mine cares.*

When it comes to my wife, I think of her as an all-purpose tester—in all areas of our lives from money to people. For instance, when I traveled as a speaker I would occasionally have a woman be flirtatious with me. (Blind women and elderly women with cataracts love me.) However, rarely did I catch it. She caught it every time and would tell me, when I obviously didn't catch on that a particular woman was being overly friendly. I didn't tell her she was nosey or she was being controlling or laugh it off and accuse her of being jealous. I stayed away from those women.

I'm sure some men would accuse me of being weak or "hen-pecked." I like how one fellow answered of himself, "I'm not hen-pecked; I just got chicken house ways." Well, call it what you will, my integrity is intact and my wife didn't need to kill me. It worked out great for both of us. Seriously, being willing to listen to her and consider her was part of the package when I married her. It might have been her imagination that some of those women were flirting with me. It doesn't matter. She deserves my consideration. I am accountable to her and she is to me. This doesn't guarantee perfection or that there will never be a failure, but it decreases the risk tremendously.

Returning to Carolyn McLeod's work, think about this,

> Trusting requires that we can, 1) be vulnerable to others (vulnerable to betrayal in particular); 2) think well of others, at least in certain domains; and 3) be optimistic that they are, or at least will be, competent in certain respects. Each of these conditions for trust is relatively uncontroversial. There is a further condition which is

controversial, however: the trustor is optimistic that the trustee will have a certain kind of motive for acting.

My suggestion for a solution here is that we should live our lives in such a way as to inspire optimism in those who have placed their trust in us.

A Different Approach

In a research article titled, "What does the brain tells us about trust and distrust," Angelika Dimoka enlightens us concerning the effect our expectation has on our attitude toward others.

> While trust is viewed as an expectation of a partner's beneficial conduct, distrust has been viewed in reciprocal terms as an "expectation of injurious action" that the trustee will not act in the trustor's best interests. Distrust reflects the trustor's expectation about the trustee's poor capabilities, negative motives, and harmful behavior and it has been viewed as lack of confidence, fear of harm, harmful and hostile intentions, and lack of care about the trustor's welfare.

Some might contend that if a person doesn't expect much out of others, he won't be disappointed. Sounds logical—except for what our attitude and words might convey to another if those low expectations are a part of how we see them. If we have low expectations of someone, he will know it, and he will also know it is because we don't think well of him. In that case I would say his motivation to meet any of our expectations would be low, if not non-existent. There is just something about knowing another has no confidence in him to make a person want to give up. It's not the same as someone who hears, "You can't do that," and is challenged to have the attitude of, "I'll show them!" What I am talking about is when one person conveys to another the thought, "You're nothing but a liar. You're a waste of time. You'll never be anything but . . ." Now, that strikes at a person's self-worth and even someone who has failed us has to believe he has enough good in him that he can be better than his failure.

Far too many times I have heard people essentially say to the person in whom they're disappointed, "There's no way I can ever win with you! No matter how hard I try you accuse me of lying or of failing in some way!" Just as trust is beneficial to a relationship, keeping the distrust in a failed relationship *under control* can also be beneficial to the relationship. I can almost hear someone arguing in protest, "So, we should trust the person who was untrustworthy?" That is not exactly what I am saying. It's natural for our brains to warn us, so to speak, when dealing with someone who has failed to be trustworthy.

My point is that when a person feels everything he or she does or doesn't do is going to result in a new interrogation then that affects her willingness to work on the relationship. If she gets no credit or appreciation for her effort at redemption or if she and her behaviors are never seen in a good light and are always suspect, expect her to give up eventually. (*One note of caution here: some may try to manipulate you with guilt and accusations of being unfair. An insincere person will usually want all restraints or all consequences removed. Set a reasonable standard and stick to it.*)

This type of exchange so often takes place in marriage relationships when there has been an affair or some other serious breach of trust. The offended person is angry and still, consciously or subconsciously, punishing the offender. He does not feel good about the person and he is determined that person will not feel good about herself until she has suffered sufficiently. Sometimes it is all about controlling the other person. In other cases it may just be irrational anger, or their chance to enjoy the status of being the "better person" in the relationship, or some other reason. The result is the same. The offender feels he or she can't succeed and gives up trying.

Balance is the key. The person who broke the trust can't be given a blank check of credibility, but neither can the person be deprived of the basic dignity and self-worth needed to motivate him or her to good works. Even if someone breaks our trust, it is not our place to punish the person. Our focus must be to rebuild the relationship if we want it to survive. As distasteful as it may sound, if we want the other person to become trustworthy again, we must treat him or her as if we see this as a real possibility.

Principles of Trust for Teens

Raising his voice in protest, Jacob questioned his parents, "Don't you trust me?" Well, as a parent of teenagers that's a tough one to answer. On one hand the answer is "yes," in that I believe you're a good kid and wouldn't intentionally go out and do anything wrong. On the other hand, the answer is "no." I don't trust that you have enough wisdom and knowledge of the world and people to just be turned loose on the world. It gets more complicated when parents have caught their children doing drugs, constantly breaking curfew, sneaking out of the house in the middle of the night, and more.

As a parent, when you are put in the position of answering the question, "Don't you trust me?" I have found some valuable insights from the writers at The Center for Parenting Education that I would like to offer.

- Trust exists on a continuum. There is a wide range of levels of trust between the two ends: full trust and no trust.
- Trust is not static: it is earned, can be damaged, and can be repaired and re-built.
- When trust is broken, the relationship is damaged.
- Trust is not always fair: Parents can trust their teens too much by not providing the guidance and limits that they still need. Parents can also under-trust by being suspicious and overly intrusive. Either extreme can set your teen up for failure and cause damage to the relationship.
- As you see improved judgment and better impulse control, you can give a little more freedom and privileges and see how he does. Often being given more privileges inspires a teen to be more responsible and trustworthy.
- One of the jobs parents have is to determine how much to trust each child in each situation; and this is not always clear-cut and obvious. You may trust her in certain situations and not others. Or you may trust your teen but worry about other people she is with who might not be reliable.
- Trust is not blind; it is based on knowledge. "I need to know where you are and what you're doing. You're on your way to being an adult, but you're not there yet and you can make some mistakes along the way that can hurt you very much. It is my job to help see that that doesn't happen."
- If trust is broken repeatedly, you may need to get help as it could be a signal that something else is going on.

And by the way, the best way to teach our children the concept of trust, the experts say is, "by modeling, not lecturing." Live it out, keep *your* promises, and you will earn their respect and trust.

Inspire Others to Be Trustworthy

I have heard it many times. The offended person in a breach of trust expresses hurt and dismay that the other person has lied, deceived, been unfaithful, or has been false in some way. The unspoken thought is often, "How could you? After all I have done for you?" What follows is a lecture on the person's lack of "loyalty." I have heard people, all with the same personality type, speak in terms of loyalty so many times while others speak in terms of "faithfulness" that I became fascinated with the possible difference in loyalty and faithfulness as it pertains to trustworthy relationships. The following is part of what I found.

I found this from Dan Sadlier. He makes the following distinctions:

> Loyalty is the commitment or dedication to a brand, person, or other entity because of something that has been experienced in the past. You are loyal to a boss who supported you financially in a past season of need. You are loyal to a mother who gave you a roof over your head as a child growing up . . . Loyalty is formed because at some point, in some season, someone or something was very good to you. It is an indebted kind of commitment based on the past.

> Faithfulness on the other hand is a different kind of dedication. Those who are faithful have full belief [or faith] in the person they are committed to. It isn't a commitment brought about my something that has happened in the past, but who that person is and who they trust that they will continue to be. There is such fullness of faith in that person that the dedication isn't based solely on something that occurred in the past, but

also in the present, and in the future. The two are very different.

One produces backward-looking, guilt-filled obligation, while the other produces a passion-infused dedication to the future. One "does" until obligation is fulfilled, the other "does" above and beyond out of joy for what was, what is, and, what has yet to come. One stays in fear, while the other goes in both freedom and gratitude.

From this, I think we can conclude that building relationships has to be above all things relational. The person we want to be trustworthy needs to be connected with us on an emotional level, and in whom we are in their lives, that a sense of faithfulness draws them to us. Hopefully this sense of faithfulness that prevents them from doing something to break our trust. People who feel "indebted" to another, but do not feel close to, accepted, or nurtured by that person will often waver in allegiance to them. Inspiring people to be trustworthy by giving things or doing things for them is a poor substitute for *being someone significant* in their lives.

In another interesting piece, Mary Jane Hurley Brant writes on the topic of *Loyalty Vs. Blind Loyalty in Families.* While loyalty is a good quality, she notes what she calls "blind loyalty" is not being a good quality in families. Here is why:

A blindly loyal person follows lockstep and unquestioningly behind the family. Often, the marching is done unconsciously because one doesn't want to upset or anger another family member—a practice of "keep the peace mentality."

Families operate on a continuum of being open with their communication or closed. Families with high functioning open systems can address any topic even when extremely painful, difficult or sensitive: loss, divorces, mental illness, secrets, alcoholism, various abuses, feelings of shame, affairs, death of beloved members, etc . . . . Individual expressions are not only permitted, they are encouraged . . .

But, this isn't the case in the closed blindly loyal family . . . heaven protect the family member who challenges the accepted family view.

Where does blind loyalty originate? Usually, it's formed in early childhood to win parental approval and love because the worse thing for a child to feel is disapproved of, unloved and unwanted. We all want to believe we had the perfect family so we ignore the imperfections and transform family issues into virtues . . . But telling ourselves that something was perfectly wonderful when it was not is emotionally unhealthy and a form of denial or repression. Those feelings don't disappear; they go underground to get projected and played out later . . . For example, the adult child who could never please mom, dad or both unconsciously feels never good enough and becomes highly reactive when criticism comes his or her way.

Let's accept that no family is perfect and most do the best they can. When we are open to this conscious shift from being a blindly loyal family member to an authentically loyal family member our families will be true places of refuge.

Where blind loyalty is demanded or expected, a dysfunctional family system is created in which lying, though not justified, may be a part of the mindset of "keeping the peace." Additionally, family members can create a false mask of sorts each wears to maintain the status quo. Ironically, honesty and openness are neither really wanted nor rewarded but instead are punished if they violate the norm for the household. The nature of trust is that of confidence, hope, faith, and reliance. Blind loyalty is false by its very nature and does nothing to build trust in a relationship.

If trusting someone who broke our trust sounds as difficult as forgiving them, I would say you have a good grasp of the subject. The nature or character of trust calls us to extend ourselves—not blindly, but with wisdom—for the sake of sharing our lives with others. It requires we be authentic and allow the other person the same opportunity. Whether we are excited about it or not, much of life's meaning is found through our relationships with others. Don't give up because of the way you may feel. Feelings can change, and yes, even people can change.

CHAPTER SIX

Committed to the Process

. . . . . .

H opefully we have laid a sufficient foundation for understanding some of the primary dynamics of human thinking and behavior involved in the issue of broken trust, and you have a good grasp of what rebuilding relational trust may ask of you. Not knowing where you may be in the process of rebuilding your relationship or even if you have started rebuilding at this point, either way I would encourage you not to be discouraged but to commit yourself to the process. Whether you are the person who broke the trust in a relationship or the person who had your trust broken, there is a process to rebuilding.

Although I will leave it to the individual to work out the process as best works for her, there are some essential components for everyone's plan. The first step on your journey is simply to make sure you are committed to the process or at least know you are trying to commit to the process. Just going through the motions or paying lip service to the process will quickly undermine any positive gains and torpedo the whole course of action. That being said, let's begin with learning to intentionally forgive and learning to intentionally trust. Next we will address learning to embrace a mindset of integrity and to purposely inspire trust in others.

Learning to Intentionally Forgive

In an article by Dr. Shann Ferch titled, *Intentional a Counseling Intervention,* he proposes a process for using intentional forgiveness to help one recover from being hurt in a relationship. I have condensed and summarized his seven-step process. The person needing to forgive is encouraged to accept and apply the following truths in utilizing intentional forgiveness:

> First, understand and accept that intentional forgiveness is a choice.
>
> Second, the choice to forgive is an immediate opportunity but forgiveness itself is a journey that involves surmounting the barricade of difficult emotions and self-preservations that will repeatedly block the desire to renew trust.
>
> Third, forgive and remember. Often people are unwilling to forgive for fear that forgiveness eliminates justice, overlooks a grievous wrong, or provides an offender with an easy way out; this misperception is clearly stated in the idiom, "forgive and forget."
>
> Fourth, teach clients to forgive for the sake of self, not the sake of the offender.
>
> Fifth, in ongoing relationships, forgiveness has two sides: one represents mercy and the process of healing and the other represents justice and the will to see responsibility taken and reoffense entirely eliminated or greatly diminished in occurrence and intensity.
>
> Sixth, consider intention versus impact. In cases involving conflict resolution (in families and marriages, with couples or with coworkers) both parties often feel wronged or wounded. In such cases, clarifying intention

and impact becomes important so that both parties may emerge with a sense of resolution and mutual reconciliation

Seventh, intentional forgiveness is a viable way to advance the relationship in the context of unresolved harmful experiences. However, forgiveness must be seen as "important and healthy."

Learning to Intentionally Trust

Maybe you were never shown you could trust others. Maybe you haven't had trustworthy people in your life for so long you are beginning to think you can't trust anyone. Maybe you're uncertain of what would inspire you to really trust another person. Maybe no one ever expressed confidence in you, and you find expressing confidence in others is difficult. Criticism—you may know criticism if that was all you heard growing up. Just a note, even though you may have turned out to be responsible doesn't mean you can inspire others to be trustworthy by criticizing them the way you were criticized.

Instead, think of yourself as a leader. The great leaders in history inspired others through raising their hopes and expectations, by appealing to their better nature. They spoke not of what others had done wrong, but of the great and noble achievements others could accomplish. We don't have to see ourselves like Martin Luther King, Jr. on the steps of the Lincoln memorial, or Moses at the Red Sea crossing in the Cecil B. DeMille movie, *The Ten Commandments,* or John F. Kennedy at his inauguration saying, "Ask not what your country can do for you . . ." Let's come back to our reality. Sometimes people just need us to believe in them.

In the book, *The SPEED of Trust: The One Thing that Changes Everything,* by Stephen M.R. Covey, he writes, "Consider your own experience. How do you feel when someone tells you, 'You can do this! You're credible. You have the character and the competence to succeed. I believe in you; I trust you.' Sometimes simply hearing those words creates all the inspiration needed for success." He continues,

> This same kind of leadership inspires trust at home. Just consider the difference it makes in the lives of children when parents tell them, "I love you. I believe in you. I trust you," and help them develop character and competence by giving them meaningful stewardships—jobs with trust—to carry out. When people at our leadership programs share their feelings about the person who has impacted them most in their lives it is most often a parent (or sometimes a teacher, coach, or a mentor at work) who believed in them when no one else did.
>
> As I've said before, the first job of a leader—at work or at home—is to inspire trust. It's to bring out the best in people by entrusting them with meaningful stewardships, and to create an environment in which high-trust interaction inspires creativity and possibility.

Do you want someone to want to earn your trust? Show him he can. Encourage him to do it—don't demand it. Show him you will not define him by his failure. Help him to believe he is redeemable. You can hold him accountable and tell him you believe in him at the same time. You can let him know you still want him in your life and that you aren't giving up, that you have hope for your relationship. All these can inspire without dispensing with accountability.

, as noted previously, we will address learning to embrace : of integrity and to know how to inspire trust in others.

A Mindset of Integrity

Honesty is what it's all about. Some were taught to lie early in their life by the example they saw. Some do it to get what they want. Some think they aren't lying because of the way they say things. A friend of mine used to jokingly say, "I'll tell you the truth a hundred different ways before I'll lie to you." Deception is lying. Half-truths are lies. Misrepresenting oneself is dishonest. You get the picture.

Now consider integrity. A person of integrity is clear in what she says and what she means. People don't question or doubt her. She is respected and usually admired. She has good relationships. Her life is never seen on "reality TV," she's never seen without her shirt on "Cops," she has never been seen in an orange jumpsuit, her spouse and children respect her. You get the picture.

People usually lie or deceive in the beginning out of fear. "Things will be better for me if I lie than if I tell the truth," they say to themselves. Eventually, they may learn it works for other things than staying out of trouble. For instance, they can get what they want that way. Amazingly, the person of integrity has a better name and a better life than the person who tries to deceive. Eventually, the deceiver is revealed and unfortunately, the end will be worse than the beginning.

A mindset of integrity is an intentional commitment to living an honest life and being authentic with and among the people who love us. It is something we choose for ourselves. No one can make us have it or choose it for us. It's a big decision that can pay big dividends.

Inspiring Trust in Others

All I suggest when trying to inspire trust is remembering you can encourage it and you can instigate it; just keep in mind, you can't make it happen. That is not to discourage you, rather to remind you that it's a process and each person moves at his or her own pace. Give people time. It will work. Let's look at a few suggestions on how.

Self-control is a surefire way of demonstrating you are trustworthy. It makes sense, if a person cannot control himself, how is anyone going to trust him? *He* doesn't even know what *he* is going to do. Correspondingly, if he demonstrates self-control, he knows better what to expect of himself and others know better what to expect of him. Research results on the correlation between a person's perceived self-control and his trustworthiness by others was published in the *Journal of Personality and Social Psychology*. The results were interesting, but not unexpected. In actual fact, "a person's perceived trait and state of self-control, in turn, influenced people's judgment of the other person's trustworthiness." To be more precise, "If you want to improve your friendships or romantic life," . . . work "on improving your self-control." "Good self-control" helps develop and maintain "'harmonious, long-lasting relationships.'"

Consistent behavior is another means of inspiring trust in others. Fundamentally, this is doing what you say you will do every time. It's not as difficult as some people think. Early in the conversation with someone, consider your ability to do or be what he or she expects of you. Ask questions if you are unclear about something so that you will know for sure to what you are agreeing. If you can't do something, don't say you will. Many instances of people's trust being broken, or of someone's being accused of lying, starts out as someone promising something he has no intention or ability to do, or he simply does not know one way or the other if he can.

Genuineness inspires trust in others. Genuineness is all about being authentic and real—not trying to constantly hide aspects of oneself or manipulate others' perception of them or of the truth. They are who they are. If they make a mistake they will own up to it. No excuses. No blaming other people. It is not, "I'm sorry, but they *(insert blaming comment)*." It is just, "Yeah, I blew that, didn't I?" kind of a response. Hear me say this with no judgment at all—just saying it like it is—if you broke someone's trust, think of the sign in the China shop, "You break it. You own it." If you broke the trust, own it. That deed belongs to you. The sooner you accept it the sooner people will begin to trust you.

One of the most sadly humorous things about people who lie and deceive others is that they think everybody is stupid enough to believe anything that comes out of their mouths. They own nothing no matter what! I am reminded of a time when I worked as a substance abuse counselor. We regularly drug tested the patients and had learned to be prepared for every attempt at deception. We even had cameras in the restrooms where urine samples were given that the nurses monitored. People still did some amazing things. One of the more unpleasant things was people dipping their sample cup in the toilet to fill it. This happened so often that we colored the water in the toilet bowl blue to eliminate one more option for those who wanted to try to deceive. Even though we had their actions on video, some would still protest.

No sooner were we satisfied we had eliminated one more thing over which we would have to challenge people than we were proven wrong. One morning a young man turned in a cup of blue water. We had not considered color-blind people. The color of the water was pointed out as was the fact he had failed his drug screen. One might think he would give it up. Not this guy, even though he watched himself dip the blue water out of the toilet on the replay from the camera and others confirmed the water was indeed blue, he never admitted, but rather continued to deny he had done it. An extreme example, but a realistic note about how foolish and untrustworthy we make ourselves look when we never take responsibility for anything we do.

All kinds of experiences will challenge our commitment to the process. All the same we must proceed to our goal—the restoration of trust in the relationship. Stay committed to the process and you can complete the restoration.

CHAPTER SEVEN

Our Initial Response to the Hurt

......

C helsea sat stunned at the revelation her husband of five years had been unfaithful to her with a woman from his workplace. He swore through tears it only happened a "few times"—as if that helped. He was desperate to soften the blow of the dark revelation. Her first thought was to throw the vase on the table beside her at him. Then there was the idea of throwing him out of the house. Instead, she just sat there weeping uncontrollably. After about an hour of crying, mixed with yelling, she began to pull it together. Always being the practical and logical one in the relationship, looking over at the picture of their little girl on the table, she took a deep breath and thought to herself, "Okay, I can do this. We can fix this. We can make it work." But then the thought, "What do I do?"

If you have recently experienced someone breaking your trust, it may feel like they broke your heart along with your trust. That being the case, it's likely that you want to know something to do that will help you process these feelings and events as soon as possible. In the following paragraphs I would offer some suggestions that may help initially.

Slow Down

Initially, simply having realistic expectations for yourself and the other person will help. Refrain from trying to move through the event on someone else's timeline. Some may identify with your experience, and relate their experience to yours, or you may relate your experience to theirs. You may encounter some who are just self-appointed authorities on the subject and will tell you something like, "You should be over that by now." Take it all as the well-meaning help it is intended to be—just don't take it to heart and don't try to let them dictate what you do. Keep healthy boundaries in place. If they push, you can respond in essence, "Thank you for your help. I will think about what you have said." Then change the subject.

Just because someone else got over a similar experience in six months or a year does not mean that timeline will work for you. In reality, others you are using as examples of how to get over the pain may not have actually worked all the way through what happened to them. Both of you may actually be assuming all is well, although if the right amount of stress were applied, the person you are using as your example may find there are lingering issues which still need to be addressed. Whatever the case, another person's experience is not *your* experience. Just because a similar hurt was inflicted in his or her life does not mean you will find healing in the same way or at the same point in time. Learn from others, but refrain from modeling your response and setting your expectations according to their experiences.

Processing what has taken place when the trust in a relationship has been broken depends greatly on the answers to a wide variety of questions. For example:

- What happened?
- What were the circumstances?

- How long did it go on?
- Was it a reoccurring event?
- How did you find out about the event?
- Why did the person apologize?
- Did the person apologize?

In the same way, processing what has happened can also be hindered by asking too many questions or seeking too many answers. Tread carefully here. Knowing every detail and every feeling and every thought of the people involved will not make the hurt go away faster. On the contrary, hearing a particular truth while the wound in your heart is fresh and deep may only serve to intensify your pain. Slow down.

Allow Room for Repentance

Allowing the person who broke your trust opportunity to atone for what he or she did may or may not be appealing. Sometimes those injured just want to "cut their losses and move on," and the last thing they want to go through is hearing apologies and excuses, nor are some particularly fond of letting the person responsible for the hurt have an opportunity to make things right. Possibly the reason is that to do so would expose them to the possibility of being hurt or disappointed again. Hence, we have the initial response of some to move on with their lives as quickly as possible. Again, as I said previously, please slow down.

True repentance on the part of the person who broke the trust is one of the most helpful offerings to the work of rebuilding trust and healing the hurt. And by repentance I mean not only being sorry, but willing to change direction in one's life and behavior. Few actions will make the other person feel inclined to be forgiving and engage in the process of rebuilding trust like having a sense there is real sorrow about the wrong that has been done. Just the same, the person who has been wronged must exercise restraint when repentance is offered. The temptation might be to respond in one of two ways:

First, to instantly absolve the person of wrongdoing or appear to do so by dismissing the wrong as "nothing" or "unimportant," or to say, "It's okay, let's not talk about it anymore," might only serve to trivialize the wrongdoing. Although one should accept the apology of someone who is genuinely repentant, don't minimize the wrong.

The conversation might sound something like this, "Thank you for apologizing. But I need you to know that even though I am going to accept your apology, what you did/said deeply hurt me and it's not okay that you did/said that, but we can move past it. I won't bring it up again and all I ask of you is that you don't do it again."

In other words, allow the full weight of the wrong to be felt and acknowledged and then release the other person by continuing the relationship as normally as possible.

Secondly, there might be a temptation to hang the other person's admission of guilt over his or her head forever. I have heard people months or years after the event justify their lack of forgiveness by essentially saying, "How can I forgive you? You admitted that you did it!" Or, "You knew what you were doing! How can I forgive you when you intentionally did that?" One would have to ask himself, with that being the case, what good was it for the person who broke the trust to admit he was wrong?

"But," some would protest, "it's impossible to forget." As I have heard people say, "I can forgive, but I can't forget." In part, this is true. Unless you or I have sustained a brain injury or begin suffering from a degenerative disease like dementia, we won't or can't forget. Just the same, this does not give us permission to hold something over someone else's head forever. *Don't use the pain of the hurt to justify a desire to hurt them back.* Let's face it. That is what it is sometimes. That memory of the wrong and the person's admission of the wrong means having power over him. It's the "ace up your sleeve." When it's needed, such as when the other person is not meeting your expectations, you can always pull that memory out and use it against him. That way you keep him in check. You retain power over the offender. This will never help preserve a relationship. In fact, it will often help destroy it.

Strive to Achieve a Balance

Although each person in a relationship must have his or her needs addressed, the relationship must be a greater priority than solely that of the individual's needs and wants. This can be the case when there are two individuals who insist on having their own way in almost all things, are demanding, narcissistic, or childish. The fallout is that there are times when these relationships are permanently destroyed, not because of the severity of the transgression, but because of the unwillingness of one or both of the people involved to give an inch.

Author of *Forgiving the Devil* and *The Essential Humility of Marriage,* Terry D. Hargrave, PhD offers some insight on this predicament as it pertains to the problem of an extramarital affair.

> For instance, if the victimizer has not been willing to take a one down position in terms of power and stabilizing the relationship, then it is doubtful that the marriage will recover from the affair. This may mean the couple divorces, but also can mean that the couple will stay married but separate emotionally. The victimized spouse may also want to hold onto the power that he or

she has in being "wronged" and continually bring up the past affair as a means of punishing the spouse. Both of these examples are usually a result of longstanding cycles of anger, aggression, or emotional distance that the couple has had in the relationship before the affair.

Working on achieving balance is not going to resolve the hurt or other issues in itself and it may prove challenging even when both people are cooperative, yet the stability it will bring to the relationship is worth all the effort. In addition, it will help set the tone for more work of restoration to be done. It's a win-win proposition for both involved. Nothing is at risk when balance is achieved.

Offer a Measure of Grace

When I say "grace" I mean mercy, understanding, or leniency. When I say a "measure" I mean a deliberate amount so as to give the other person hope, but not so much as to imply quickly dismissing it. Remember, we are talking about an initial response while the hurt or disappointment is still fresh and there has not been enough to resolve the issue. This is not about keeping the other person "on the hook" or to keep them guessing or in the dark as to whether or not you are going to forgive them. Only to contend that slamming the door on any possibility of forgiveness or the likelihood of it will only serve to close you off emotionally to the other person and to discourage him or her from trying to make amends. The gift of hope is in the hand of the person wronged. Giving the gift to the other person is your choice.

Confide in a Select Few

Looking for emotional support is natural and can be helpful, but the temptation to run to multiple family and friends with details of the hurt will often complicate the future of the relationship. Worse still is to post information about your relationship problems on social network sites. Such has been the flawed decisions of people desperate to find support, sympathy, or understanding. What happens is that people invariably choose sides bringing further division, or someone gets their feelings hurt because someone wants to remain neutral or stay out of the fray and won't choose sides.

What's worse is when the vultures sweep in and try to make an easy meal of one of the people in the troubled relationship. That's right. It happens. When the issue is broadcast for the world to hear, on occasion, someone who always wanted to "get with" one of the people having problems will start up a relationship with that person under the guise of being sympathetic. Soon they meet "just to talk" and soon things get out of hand and more harm is done to the relationship. Again, if you find things moving faster than you can make sense of them—slow down.

Slowing down doesn't limit our options—it may increase them. Slowing down doesn't mean we have committed to a plan of action we can't reverse—going too fast often does. Slowing down and not making rash decisions is always beneficial in relationships. When we slow down we can see the other person more accurately, we can allow time for change to take place, we can allow time for God to answer our prayers, and we don't have to try to undo actions or try to take back the things we have said.

CHAPTER EIGHT

Admitting One's Guilt

. . . . . .

Admitting one's guilt, if done for the good of any relationship, must be done to seek forgiveness from the other person so as to attain forgiveness or to make things right. Admitting one's guilt and apologizing should not be about easing one's guilty conscience. This would likely cause the other person to feel more hurt—first, because of the wrong done to him or her and, second, because the one doing the confessing presents himself as more concerned about his own feelings rather than the offended person's feelings.

Usually, there are at least two different situations under which people typically admit they are guilty of some transgression. The first would be when they have been caught. The second would be when there is a need to make things right and the other person may or may not know of the wrongdoing. If you're the one who had to admit guilt in a breach of trust, there are a few things you need to know.

Your Sincerity May Be Questioned

The first, being "caught in the act" scenario is the more difficult of the two. No matter how sorry one might be and no matter how much one sincerely apologizes, the fact the person is apologetic because she *was* caught will almost always cast doubt on her sincerity—at least in the eyes of the person who caught her. No doubt you have heard people say, "They're not sorry. They're just sorry they got caught!" Then the skeptical person's logic kicks in, "If she had not gotten caught she would have just kept on doing it." This is where the skeptical person becomes judgmental and acts as if he/she knows the other person's heart. This is not advised. No matter what others choose to say and do, the person who was "caught" must commit himself to earning again the right to be trusted.

Many people say or do wrong things and then decide to discontinue that behavior even though they were not caught. Just the same, people will usually be skeptical about the one who is caught and then apologizes. So what is that person to do? First, whether caught or not, stop doing what is offensive or wrong. Second, consider apologizing, coming clean, even if one has not been caught. In most, if not all cases, it is the best thing to do.

I say most all cases, though there are actually exceptions. I am not advocating just blurting out one's transgressions anywhere to anyone and anytime. For example, if you felt bad about accidently running over your dying grandmother's beloved cat, it might be best to keep that to yourself rather than easing *your* conscience by whispering in a dying woman's ear, "I killed your cat; sorry, Grandma." In the grand scheme of things, there are more important things to consider. On the other hand, if a woman who is about to marry her long-time boyfriend finds out she is pregnant, but knows the baby might not be his, she needs to tell her fiancé as soon as possible and definitely before the wedding.

Finally, one should use discretion as to the time and place one chooses to offer a confession and apology. For instance, don't do as one man I heard about who confessed for the first time to his wife of an affair he had been having—in front of the whole church! Or as in other instances I have heard about, in front of family or to family members or friends before confessing to one's spouse. In most cases where hurt and wrongs have taken place between two people, a good rule of thumb is to keep people outside your relationship, outside your relationship.

Handling the Confession

It's easy to handle admitting one's guilt incorrectly. This calls for foresight. Do it the wrong way and you could look like you're seeking sympathy, making excuses, trying to gain the support of others, just doing it because you were caught, even trying to embarrass the person you have hurt. Do it the right way and the relationship has the best chance of surviving and being healed. Confessing one's guilt is tough enough without having one's sincerity questioned. So, for the one confessing, think things through, get some wise counsel, and decide what the best way is for the person you have hurt to hear about what you have done. It is not just about you.

For the person receiving the apology, it is also easy to handle an apology the wrong way. The thing to remember is that if someone exercises the courage to confess a great wrong, keep in mind that having his or her sincerity questioned will likely be frustrating and may lead to more hesitation about being forthcoming with more information. Do you want the truth, the whole truth, and nothing but the truth? Even if you have doubts—listen. Ask questions. However, this is not the time for putting that person on trial. She is admitting her guilt. The trial is over. Now is the time to set the tone for the days ahead when the time will come for addressing the consequences for what has been done.

Admit, Acknowledge, Own Up to It

In an article titled in part, *"But I Said I Was Sorry"* researchers looked at the importance of apologies in relation to the expectations of the victim. Their findings were interesting in that, "Despite the many potential benefits of apologies, it is clear that people are not always satisfied with the specific apology content they receive . . . To truly arouse forgiveness, apologies must also include the specific components that the victim needs to hear." In a few words, as I would say it, we can't just say we're sorry, we have to say it the right way. My version didn't sound as academic, but you get the point.

Returning to the article, the researchers continue, "Across such fields as law, sociology, and psychiatry, scholars have focused on three apology components that are particularly relevant to this issue. These are: offers of compensation, expressions of empathy, and acknowledgments of a violated rule/norm." People want to know that we know why they were hurt, why what we did was wrong, how we plan to make it up to them, and they want to know we feel badly about doing what we did. *It helps them believe we won't do it again.*

In addition, when it comes to admitting one's guilt, it shouldn't be done little by little. We have all probably read of or seen news reports about politicians or other famous people who were accused of an inappropriate relationship with someone or of some unethical behavior connected with their jobs. Immediately, the damage control "experts" go to work helping the person craft a well-written press release that essentially denies any wrongdoing without actually explaining or denying anything specific. Often they imply they were "unaware" of any wrongdoing or unaware why their actions would be called into question. They're either waiting to see what people actually know before defending themselves or looking for what they call "deniability."

When they can't plead ignorance of the events or escape the obvious truth, they will begin to let the admissions come out, but only a little at a time. For example, they might say, "Yes, I was there, but not with that person." Then next week or next month, "Yes, I was there with them, but nothing happened. I barely spoke to them." At a later date, as the story falls apart, "Okay, I was there with them, and I was flirting and dancing with them, but nothing happened at the party." As you can imagine, there will be a great deal of concern there is more to the story that has not been revealed. These offerings of truth in bits and pieces and only as required will only chip away at the other person's confidence that one is being truthful. This can also serve to reopen the wound repeatedly. By the time the entire confession is made trust is gone and everyone is still waiting for the next revelation. Even when all appears to be revealed, the person is viewed with suspicion as if he or she is still hiding something because of the manner in which the explanation was given.

Apologies Work—Just Not Quickly

Some worry, and rightly so, that what they did cannot or will not be forgiven. This fear often comes to mind when the tearful sincere apology doesn't make everything okay or when the other person does not appear to be willing to accept it. My advice: As a former president was known to have said, "Stay the course." If you mean it and are genuinely sorry, don't give up. Initial reactions can change. Professors Dr. Laura May and Dr. Warren Jones found in part that "sincere apologies can aid in the eventual reconciliation of two individuals after some hurtful incident, regardless of the severity of the event and the intensity of the initial hurt response." Another point to remember at this time is the person who has been deceived and betrayed has been hurt deeply. The person may feel shaken at his or her core. Remember, the betrayed person—parent, friend, spouse, fiancé—often thought they had a relationship based on trust and mutual respect. At this point, in a state of shock and disbelief, the same people will often question the validity of everything and everyone. One might hear them say, "If I can't trust you then . . ." or "If our relationship was a lie all along, how can I know what is real?" *This is one more reason why saying, "Sorry" doesn't make it all okay right away. Give it time.*

Humility Is Important

Common sense dictates that an attitude of humility will make it more likely one will forgive and be forgiven. On the other hand, an arrogant, narcissistic, or unforgiving attitude will cause a person to either refuse to apologize, because what he believed what he did was really provoked or caused by someone else's words or actions, or because he felt entitled in some way to take that action. He may refuse to accept the apology of another because he sees himself as someone who "would never do such a thing," and thus the behavior of the other person is so contemptible, forgiveness is not possible or is excessively difficult. Consequently, humility on the part of both people, and/or all people involved, is essential to making the apology/forgiveness paradigm work.

In an article on *"Relational Humility"* in the *Journal of Personality Assessment,* it was that humility was an essential part of the process for the one offering an apology and another offering forgiveness:

Previous theory and research has focused on humility of the victim, proposing that humility can promote empathy and dissipate feelings of disgust and moral superiority toward the offender. For example, self-reports of humility have been positively associated with trait forgivingness. Moreover, victims have been found to be more likely to forgive when they considered themselves capable of committing a similar offense. Whereas these studies focused on humility in the victim, we focused on the degree to which the victim judged the offender as possessing humility. In both studies, perceiving an offender as humble was positively related with greater forgiveness.

Through the years I have seen it over and over again. As a rule, people who are arrogant will neither ask for forgiveness nor give it to others. In many cases it is because, for the arrogant or narcissistic person to offer or ask for forgiveness would be to give up power over the other person or to give power to the other person. This person will not tolerate the idea of being indebted to another nor will he give up the opportunity to try to rule the other person. If you are not willing to truly forgive or to ask for forgiveness, you may lack humility. It's just a thought.

Shame Is a Factor

Shame is a tough feeling to live with when you are trying to move forward and be a better person. It feels worse if a person previously had a sense of pride—the good kind of pride—in herself. Pride can be a major problem if it has grown to the point of one having an inflated ego. Shame can be a problem at almost any point if it takes up residence in our minds. The feeling and sense one has fallen is hard to escape. Just don't ever believe it's impossible to escape it.

One of my favorite writers, Max Lucado, posted the following on his blog:

> Pride and shame. You'd never know they are sisters. They appear so different. Pride puffs out her chest. Shame hangs her head. Pride boasts. Shame hides. Pride seeks to be seen. Shame seeks to be avoided. But don't be fooled, the emotions have the same parentage. And the emotions have the same impact. They keep you from your Father.
> Pride says, "You're too good for him."
> Shame says, "You're too bad for him."
> Pride drives you away.
> Shame keeps you away.
> If pride is what goes before a fall, then shame is what keeps you from getting up after one.

Did you catch that last part? "Shame is what keeps you from getting up after [a fall]." Shame will keep us away from the God who loves us and the people who love us. Shame is a self-imposed prison cell constructed out of our embarrassment. The sad thing is that it holds people bound for years and yet its prison bars are only as strong as we allow them to become.

Moving on is part of the healing process, even for those weighed down with feelings of shame. Feeling badly for doing something wrong shows good moral judgment and produces a remorseful heart and behavior. Feeling badly about oneself is not as productive. Initially after breaking the bond of someone's trust it would be normal to feel badly for what one has done and to be a little down on oneself—even to question one's own character. Nevertheless, to stay there, dwelling on what a terrible person one might be accomplishes nothing just as the person we hurt constantly reminding us of our failure would accomplish nothing good.

It's Still a Two-Way Street

Lest being repentant or sorry for one's actions and asking for forgiveness become all about the person needing forgiveness, one must also seek to understand the other person's perspective. To do this one must listen to the person who is hurt or betrayed. Empathy, or compassion, and understanding of the other person are essential to making amends to a relationship. Consider what Dr. Henry Cloud has to say about truly listening to the heart and needs of others as one seeks to build a relationship where trust is the foundation.

> Where there is a failure in empathy and understanding, trust is not built. People who devalue other people's thoughts, feelings, and opinions do not get inside their hearts. We must listen, validate, hear, and communicate that we have heard someone before we try to tell them "what is right." Listening first causes that to happen.
>
> In business, marriage, friendship, or any other arena, trust is built when someone has the capacity to really listen to the other person's reality and value it. When bosses listen to employees, or to customers, loyalty is built. When spouses listen to their spouses instead of getting defensive and telling them what reality is, intimacy is deepened. When parents listen to their children, they get inroads into their hearts. When negotiators listen to the other side, they are able to resolve impasses.

> When people do not listen, and invalidate other
> people's opinions or feelings, the other people will
> disconnect, find someone who will listen, and often
> turn against them.

Imagine, I did you wrong, broke your trust, and then my deed came back to haunt me. I realize I have to apologize to you and ask for your forgiveness. Following through on what I know I need to do, I acknowledge my wrong and ask you to forgive me. In turn, you say that you will, but then begin to explain to me how I hurt you and the problems it has caused for you. What if I stop you and roar back at you, "What do you want from me? I said I was sorry!"

You respond in confusion and hurt and try to explain, "I was just trying to tell you how I felt!"

Again I blow up saying, "I know I hurt you, that's why I said I was sorry! Why can't you just let it be? Why do we have to talk everything to death?"

Imagine how you would be feeling in this situation. So much for the apology I gave. In fact, it is likely you would feel that my apology was really all about relieving my conscience and not because I cared about you. Why? Because I didn't listen to you, that's why. By my not listening to your feelings about what I had done, I made my request for forgiveness all about me.

In light of my response, what are the chances we are going to have our relationship restored? Slim to none are the chances I would say. I could plead all day long, "But I said I was sorry!" It won't change a thing. On the other hand, had I just listened to what you had to say with concern and followed your comments with something like, "That's why I am so sorry, because I know I hurt you so much," the relationship would have had a much greater chance of being healed. As you can see, for the person offering the apology, it's about much more than saying, "Sorry."

Forgiving Oneself Is Acceptable

It may seem that beating oneself up and not allowing yourself to forgive yourself might be the right thing to do if you are feeling horrible about what you have done. In fact, I have encountered people over the years who have never forgiven themselves for past deeds. The weight of their misdeeds hangs over them like a black cloud or else they wear their failure like a martyr's crown. They're "messed up" they say—not that they "messed up" but that *they are* messed up. Maybe for them it's like paying penance. It's their way of atoning for what they did. After all, they seem to reason, *I made someone hurt and unhappy, why shouldn't I hurt and be unhappy?*

My question is, "What good does that really accomplish?" In reality, it does nothing. In fact, they may actually hurt the other person more. Let me explain. Pat and Charlie had been married for fifteen years when Charlie's gambling problem hit the crisis level. The result was that Pat and Charlie lost their home to the bank that foreclosed on them due to Charlie's not making the house payment. They were both devastated. Pat was initially furious, but with time came to forgive Charlie. Charlie even quit gambling. Unfortunately, he took up drinking. The more depressed he became the more he drank. The more he drank the more depressed he got.

Pat would plead with him to quit. He would cry and tell her he felt so bad about being the cause of losing the house. Drinking seemed to ease the pain, he reasoned to her and himself. Things did not turn out well. Coming home from a bar late one night, Charlie was killed in a one-vehicle wreck due to his being drunk. Pat was alone now. It was as if twice Charlie hurt her. He didn't want to, he didn't mean to, but that is how it turned out. All Pat could think about was that if Charlie had just forgiven himself, as she had forgiven him, by now they would have had a new home and would have grown old together. Charlie accomplished nothing good by not forgiving himself.

Time to Prove Yourself

It not only takes time to prove oneself, this is the time to prove oneself. (We are going to talk more about this in coming chapters.) It's only natural that after a person expresses regret and asks for forgiveness, it is not uncommon for the other party to take a wait-and-see attitude. Maybe it is our cynical society. Maybe it is the fact the other person has been disillusioned in the past by someone's insincere apology. We don't always know why people question us; we just know that they do if we have a poor track record. While I do recognize that with some people the past may be an indicator of what could happen again, I am also a firm believer that for people who are committed to change, the past does not dictate the future. For now all you need to know is *it's time* and *there is time*.

CHAPTER NINE

To Whom the Confession
is Being Made

. . . . . .

W hen someone has broken our trust we feel it will help us get over the hurt if we "know everything." We want to make sense of it all. I guess it's just human to want to know—like the old newspaper reporter—the "who, what, when, where, and why"—and we quiz the other person as if doing a story on recent events. When we do this it is likely that we are allowing ourselves to obsess. Nevertheless, this is a time we must exercise restraint.

To begin with, the truth may not come close to justifying or making the wrong seem to have some rhyme or reason. Sometimes people just do stupid things. A classic example would be a man or woman having an adulterous affair. The hurt of the betrayal is bad enough when the relationship has been in trouble for years or been severely lacking for a long time. However, when the betrayed husband or wife, was under the impression their marriage was "fine" and felt "in love" with their mate who betrayed them, there is little, if anything that will help make the affair make sense. It is like being blindsided or taking a hit that seems to come from nowhere.

The shock itself is enough. Add to that the question of "why" and you have a mix that makes making sense of the event all but impossible. There is the struggle of knowing the other mate put himself in that position, pursued it to some degree for some time, and made the decision at some point to act on the temptation and more. However, the thought of her marriage relationship being disregarded by the other person is just too much to easily reconcile.

With all that in mind, let me take you back to the truth that all this will not be easily reconciled. If you have been hurt, ask yourself, "What would it really take for me to be able to say, 'Oh, that makes sense'"? It's not going to happen, is it? Yes, you do need to know some things like, "What he was thinking?" and "Why did he choose to engage in the affair?" These questions can give insight into what needs to be addressed in order to repair the relationship. Likewise, the person who had the affair needs to do some real soul-searching as to what was going on in his or her head and heart that would have led to those decisions. Whether or not to continue the marriage relationship, that defect in integrity needs to be addressed before entering into a relationship with another.

All that said, we come to where one should draw the line in asking questions to make sense of the hurt. Seeking out too many details about what happened can develop into a multitude of what we call "triggers." These "triggers" are events, places, dates, etc., that serve to remind us of the wrong—or trigger our memory of the event. An example might be to want to know every place an unfaithful spouse met with the person in secret. It sounds like it is important, but it can cause future hurt. Let me explain. Let's say a person wants to know every restaurant where the two met for their rendezvous. The adulterer tells the spouse. Now, every time the person passes by any of those restaurants he or she is reminded of the affair.

An exception would be when it is much more personal in nature, such as the question of did the spouse bring the other person into the home? I think whether or not an adulterous act took place in their home or in their own bedroom would be of importance because that possibly indicates a much more serious transgression and violation due to the lack of respect for the marriage conveyed by using one's own home.

All that being said, the need to know, to somehow make sense of it all, can be a risky pursuit that should be taken slowly and should not become a prerequisite for forgiving a person, because forgiveness is as much or more for the person offering it as it is for the person needing it. As Lewis Smedes reminds us, "Forgiving is not having to understand. Understanding may come later, in fragments, an insight here and a glimpse there, after forgiving." Continue on the journey. Take your time. Don't become despondent or discouraged because you can't make sense of the hurt now. Many times a greater distance from the hurt will provide a clearer view. Just don't rush to put distance between you and the event by denying the significance of your feelings and trying to just pretend everything is "okay" when in your heart it is not okay.

Something Was Lost

It would almost be impossible for a significant breach of trust to take place in a relationship without the innocent party experiencing grief. Yes, I said grief. Anytime we lose something we experience grief. When someone we trusted or loved breaks our trust we lose the innocence of that relationship, the close feeling toward that person, confidence, and more. It is enough to leave a person feeling disillusioned and brokenhearted. Many feel sad or stunned. Some try to rationalize what happened and make sense of it all. Some only remember feeling angry. These are all genuine feelings and also feelings associated with the grief process.

Something has been lost and it will take you time to grieve that which has been lost. Elisabeth Kübler-Ross is credited with first proposing what is known as the "Five Stages of Grief," in her 1969 book *On Death and Dying*. The five stages can usually be applied to any situation in which a person has experienced loss. Consider the following five stages and how we might apply them to the issue of a significant breach of trust:

1. **Denial and Isolation**—"I can't believe this has happened. Surly they did not do that."
2. **Anger**—"This is wrong! I demand to know why! You have to make this right."
3. **Bargaining**—"Maybe if I had just . . ."
4. **Depression**—"If I can't trust them, what's the use in trusting anyone?"
5. **Acceptance**—"People aren't perfect. I've learned from this. It's time to move on."

Getting Past the Anger

People often get hung up in two areas more than any other. The first is in the area of anger. The second is in depression or sadness. What often confuses people is that their anger seems to circle back on them repeatedly, making them doubt they have forgiven or are forgiving. This is actually normal and doesn't necessarily mean that at all. Therapist Mira Kirshenbaum, whose husband confessed to being involved with another woman thirty years ago, writes in part about the need to keep one's anger under control in her book, *I Love You But I Don't Trust You: The Complete Guide to Restoring Trust in*

Your Relationship. Her advice to the injured spouse is, "The less anger we indulge in, the faster healing happens." She explains, "One man who cheated on his wife told the therapist he understood his wife had a right to be angry, 'It's just that her anger is bottomless. I just can't help thinking, 'What's the point?'" Kirshenbaum suggests the reason for venting one's anger is often that, "We need to know if the person who has betrayed us really understands how much pain they have caused us."

Getting Past the Sadness

The other area in which people often get hung up is sadness or depression. These feelings must be voiced and even wrestled with at times, acknowledging or admitting your feelings in order to process them. Suppressing them will not help nor will living in a state of denial. I'm often concerned when I see someone dealing with a major breach of trust in her relationship, and yet she's "fine" when asked about it. I call it the "just fine" syndrome. In some families the members are always "fine" no matter what. So much has been emotionally swept under the rug there is a mountain in the middle of the room. The person(s) is often codependent and can have that faraway look in her eyes that lets others know she has tried to disconnect in some way from the pain. Additionally, these are the people who, because they have held their feelings in for so long, explode one day with an emotional outburst.

I'm not advocating one should constantly dwell on the past events—just not ignore them. The grief or sadness must be processed. In *Torn Asunder*, Dave Carder explains what this means in the instance of infidelity in a marriage. He explains,

This grief process is similar to grieving the death of a spouse. Violated spouses do indeed report many responses that parallel those of widows:

- They feel abandoned by their mate.
- They feel alone in their grief.
- They feel as if they could have done something to prevent this.
- They feel like a marked person. They don't fit in with normal couples anymore.
- They have a lot of unfinished business with their spouse that is now off-limits or has been overshadowed by what has occurred.
- They feel terrified of the future.
- They feel they should be doing better than they are for the time that they've been in it.
- They will even pretend nothing has happened (such as the widow who sets a plate for the lost partner at the dinner table).

Grieving is important, but it is even more important to know what you are grieving for. Some find it helpful to list the losses on paper. I recommend that you try that, being as transparent and honest as you can.

That being said, let me be quick to add that he is not advocating being as "transparent and honest" as one can with just anyone or just anywhere. The technology boom has led to a great deal of progress and great advances in our world—just not in the area of true relationships. The Internet and social networking sites have allowed many to be too open and left many a little too exposed and vulnerable to hurt. A broken heart must be handled with care. This is where texting, "tweeting", and going on social networking sites do not help and may even make the hurt worse.

Stacy Notaras Murphy explains in an article titled, "What becomes of the brokenhearted?" how in our society brokenhearted people are often "retraumatized" after they have found themselves brokenhearted over events such as an affair. Citing several sources she explains that some experience "symptoms similar to posttraumatic stress and grief" by re-experiencing the hurt through "conversations, images or events related to the breakup" and even "experience physical or emotional distress triggered by moments that run the gamut from calendar dates to social media postings." This all goes to show that airing your hurt for the world to hear and see may be counterproductive to getting beyond the hurtful events of one's life. A trusted friend, pastor, or professional counselor would be a better choice.

Getting Past the Disillusionment

When a person has really invested in a relationship on an emotional level, whether it is in an intimate relationship or just believing deeply in a person's character and intentions, and then are disillusioned by the person's behavior it can cause a person to struggle a bit. During these stages it is not uncommon for people to isolate themselves, question themselves, others in general, or even God. When there was a specialness or closeness to the relationship that equals a significant loss in one's life, she may respond with feeling sad, numb, or irritable and give the impression she is inconsolable. There's a good reason. What was is gone. The past can't be undone.

Nevertheless, it does not have to end there. Whether in death or disappointment most people move on past their losses no matter what they may be, and go on to create new relationships, but they do it by processing the events and their feelings. We humans have the ability to sort things out, make sense of them, learn from them, and create something new for ourselves in which we can invest ourselves—especially when it comes to relationships. No one has to want that, or feel comfortable with that, though it is possible. Maybe refraining from entering any new relationships for a while or taking a slower, more passive approach to pursuing an existing relationship might be helpful in regaining one's emotional footing. However, one must be careful to not become isolated or build emotional walls. This would only serve to deepen those sad or cynical feelings.

Don't Allow the Sadness to Turn to Bitterness

Forgiveness is difficult enough at times without the emotional turmoil that often complicates the process. It is difficult to explain bitterness to someone who has never had it take hold of his heart and mind. It is more of an experience than a thought or idea. Bitterness is like the lasting effects of a wasp sting. There is the initial sharp pain followed by the swelling and throbbing that lingers as one's body tries to deal with the poison injected into it from the stinger of the wasp. Bitterness is like the swelling and soreness that follows a painful sting. Yes, the sting is painful, but more agonizing is the hurt caused by the lingering effect of the poison. Bitterness is the hurt that lingers.

One of the biggest problems with bitterness is that most never see it growing until it has taken root. Maybe that is why the writer of the book of Hebrews, in the New Testament, warned of bitterness. In the twelfth chapter he wrote, "Pursue peace with all people, and holiness, without which no one will see the Lord: looking carefully lest anyone fall short of the grace of God; lest any root of bitterness springing up cause trouble, and by this many become defiled"

(Hebrews 12:14-15 NKJV). The writer knew the potential for the "root of bitterness" to "spring up" in us if our relationships with others went sour and became filled with hurt, so he warns the reader to watch for or be careful not to allow "any" root of bitterness to take hold. It's good advice. It's just tough to do.

Allow me one more analogy in trying to describe bitterness for those who may have never really experienced it. As has been said, bitterness is not something most people will see coming. Often they are too distracted by the anger they feel. It is almost as if one wakes up one morning and realizes bitterness has taken hold. As such, when I think of the manner in which bitterness creeps into someone's life I think of bitterness being like mold growing on the soul. Yes, it's that unpleasant and distasteful to imagine.

If you have ever lived in a damp, humid climate or have experienced flood, you know all that moisture can cause the growth of mold at an alarming rate. To compound the problem, mold often grows out of sight, behind walls, under floors, in ductwork, anywhere there is an absence of light and clean, fresh air. Many homes have been ruined by mold while the homeowner has lived in the home unaware of what was taking place out of sight. It grows imperceptibly at first; however, the mold will eventually make itself known. Mold has an odor to it. It also releases its particles into the air and can be breathed into the homeowner's lungs, making the person sick. Once discovered it is difficult to get rid of and can require extensive work. In the worst-cases, the home is no longer livable and must be torn down. The only really good news about mold is that it is almost always preventable if one is vigilant.

All this comparison is meant to drive home the truth that bitterness must be avoided at all costs when trying to rebuild a relationship. Bitterness is the "mold" that threatens to destroy your home. Yes, the lies threatened your home, so did the deceitful behaviors, as did the personal failures. But in most cases these can be addressed—if bitterness doesn't take hold. Bitterness prevents forgiveness from taking place. Bitterness makes healthy relationships impossible. Bitterness refuses to give trust another chance. Bitterness is a corrosive that eats away at goodwill and holds the injured person in a pit of his own making.

Bitterness Can Ruin Future Blessings

Lynn was surprised to find out about the effects of bitterness because she had always been a forgiving person and had always been willing and able to accept that people make mistakes. After all, "No one is perfect," she would often say. That was until she met and worked with Tammy. Lynn and Tammy both worked for the billing department at a large medical service provider. Tammy had only been with the company about a year, but appeared to be a hard worker and had already had a couple of small promotions. Lynn had been with the company for over five years and was Tammy's supervisor. They worked well together. Tammy was efficient and Lynn loved efficiency. She was a by-the-book kind of person, someone who always wanted things to be "right"—there would be no "fudging" on the billing of insurance claims. Accuracy was honesty and honesty was essential.

You can probably imagine Lynn's dismay and upset the day Tammy came to her with some paperwork with which she had concerns. It appeared that the head of their department, Tracy, had been "adjusting" some of the claims by adding to the list of services provided. The result was the insurance companies were paying for more services than actually took place. The increased revenue had made Tracy look good and she had been commended a number of times for her work. Tracy had graciously attributed the increased revenue to the efficiency of her staff. Whatever the case, Tracy was now in line for a major promotion. What was Lynn to do? There she and Tammy sat with the proof—in black and white—that Tracy was doing something that was illegal.

Wanting to give Tracy the benefit of the doubt or at least give Tracy the opportunity to do what was right, she felt she should talk with Tracy about what Tammy had brought to her. Maybe she was unaware of something. Tammy was in complete agreement. So, after discussing it at lunch, they went in to talk with Tracy. After Lynn explained what had been found, she paused to hear what Tracy would say—hoping for the best. Tracy was obviously upset and her face was flushed red with apparent anger. Turning to Tammy sitting quietly through the meeting thus far, she asked, "What do you think about what Lynn has just said?" "Well, I don't know," Tammy said quietly and tentatively before continuing, "It's a lot to take in; this is the first I have heard about any of this."

Lynn turned and looked at Tammy with her mouth falling open and a look of utter disbelief on her face. She wanted to call her out and scream, "You liar!" However, she was so stunned she could not form a response. Turning back to Tracy, she just stared, stunned and bewildered at what had just taken place. "I don't know what you're trying to pull here, Lynn, bringing Tammy in here with you. Are you trying to make me look bad? You have a lot of nerve coming in here making these accusations! You obviously haven't done your homework. I think you both need to get back to work."

With that, Lynn and Tammy got up and walked quietly out of Tracy's office. Tammy started to say something, but Lynn just held up her hand waving her off and quickly headed for the restroom where she proceeded to break down in tears.

Tammy burst in the restroom and blurted out, "I was afraid of losing my job!"

It no longer mattered at that point. The damage was done. Tracy began making it more uncomfortable and difficult for Lynn at work in the weeks to come and finally Lynn had enough. She left the company when she found a good job at another company and tried to put the whole thing behind her. She did pretty well at that until she saw Pat, a woman she had worked with in the previous job and Pat said to her, "Well, I guess you've heard?"

"Heard what?" Lynn asked.

"Tammy was promoted to your old job," Pat informed her.

Lynn was stunned and just stood there speechless.

"Yep, she's got your old job, your title, and even your old office," Pat added.

Lynn mumbled something and then excused herself, telling Pat she had to go, but inside she was furious. She had tried to do what was right and the person doing the wrong was still getting away with it, while she had to change jobs! *To add insult to injury*, she thought to herself, *The person who made the original accusation against Tracy came out of it unscathed and is sitting in my old office with my job!*

This is about the point where Lynn's bitterness took root. Eventually Tracy was caught in her wrongdoing and she took Tammy down with her. But this did little to alleviate the bitterness Lynn felt in her heart. Ironically, she was better off than if she had stayed at her old company. Things were going great, but even the newly found success was spoiled by her growing bitterness. At this point, Lynn needed only to focus on getting past the bitterness she felt, *not* on restoring a relationship with Tammy. Sometimes one just needs to move on. In fact, Tammy was one of those people with whom a trust-filled relationship is unlikely because Tammy is best described as a chameleon of sorts—always willing to change her colors for her own benefit. She has a "whatever-it-takes" to survive mentality.

Moving On

For Lynn, as with many others who struggle with bitterness, it grew and took hold in her heart and mind before she knew it and once it had taken root it was difficult to dig up and cast out. Ironically, for most that are filled with bitterness over such betrayals, all they want is to move on with their lives. Few people enjoy bitterness though it may appear that way at times. What can happen is the event comes to define the person. The person feels incapable or unknowing of how to move on with their lives. No amount of apologizing by the offender, no amount of determining to forgive, or new blessings flowing into their lives seems to help. They are stuck.

I was stuck in bitterness once due to a betrayal so distasteful that left me grappling to come to terms with what had happened. The level of bitterness was so great it tainted my whole life. Rather than go into the hurt I will give you the secret I found for getting unstuck. At least it worked for me. The truth was something that occurred to me when I heard a minister preaching from the Old Testament passage from the book of Ruth. There is the story of two women, Ruth and Naomi, found in the first chapter that you may have heard quoted in marriage ceremonies or taught in church. This is the story of Ruth and Naomi—the young woman who would not abandon her mother-in-law in her time of need.

In the story, Ruth had married one of Naomi's two sons. All was well. Naomi had two sons, two wonderful daughters-in-law, and a good husband. However, evidently not too long after her family seemingly became complete, Naomi's husband died and both of her sons were killed, leaving Ruth, her sister-in-law, and Naomi widowed. Naomi became embittered over the loss of her sons and husband. Likewise, their lives became much more difficult due to trying to obtain the necessities of life, and in the twentieth verse, Naomi is heard telling those around her to no longer call her "Naomi" but rather to call her "Mara" which means "bitter."

She was so bitter she actually changed her name to "Bitter." Have you been there? Many have. Thankfully, that's not the end of the story. Ruth, of whom it was said in the fourth chapter, was better to Naomi than "seven sons" would have been, would not leave Naomi, and later followed her from the country of Moab in search of the necessities of life. This is where she met a wealthy man named Boaz. Ruth eventually married Boaz and had a son called, Obed, who became the father of Jesse who was the father of King David. But during all this time Naomi had remained bitter until a life-changing event—the birth of a grandchild! When her grandson was born, she found a new purpose in life. She was needed to help care for him and to love him and nurture him. This is where she became "Naomi" once again, which by the way means "Pleasant." This is where she found the pleasantness of life again and was able to release the bitterness of the past.

As for me, when I found a new purpose, something in which I could invest my life and talents, "something to go to," I was able to move on from the hurt of betrayal and, as the bitterness began to go away, the pleasantness began to return to my life.

CHAPTER TEN

Now that the Door is Open

· · · · · ·

Based on the assumption that at some point, almost all people who have had a break in a personal relationship, will at least consider continuing that relationship, I would encourage wise counsel before moving forward. Just because apologies were offered does not mean all is well. Work needs to be done in the relationship to prevent this from happening again.

This new starting point may have been reached through tearful apologies or the simple necessity to continue the relationship for some reason—at least for the present. This gives us an open door or an opportunity to mend the relationship. The value of this opening can be priceless and should not be underestimated. Now is the time to begin the restoration process or at least explore the possibilities. The hurt may be fresh and the temptation may be to withdraw, but resist this temptation and move toward one another. No one is saying to ignore the wrong, just play nice, or pretend nothing happened. Just move toward one another if given the chance.

Although the following truths would be useful in restoring trust in almost any relationship, for the time being we will focus on addressing one of the most damaging breaches of trust—that of marital infidelity. In this instance, restoring trust in order to preserve the relationship may be motivated initially by a need to stay in the relationship "for the sake of the children," or out of financial necessity, or even because of a religious belief against divorce. In these cases, forgiveness and restoration of the relationship loom above the couple like an insurmountable mountain peak. We have spoken a great deal about the importance of forgiveness, but complete forgiveness can often take a long time. This can be problematic because many relationships will never survive to see forgiveness unless some semblance or measure of trust is restored as soon as possible.

For the person who broke the trust in the relationship, you have little control over the other person's decision to forgive or ability to work through the hurt. Yet, there is one thing over which you have a great deal of control and that is *what you do* in the rebuilding of trust. No, you can't make the other person trust you any more than you can make him forgive you. Just the same, what you choose to do, how you choose to live your life, your attitude toward him, can make a huge difference in whether or not he will find it easier to trust you again or more difficult to learn to trust you again.

A Door of Opportunity

The following three tasks we will cover are primarily the responsibility of the one who broke the trust. I say "primarily" in all areas because no one person can repair a relationship on his or her own. Everyone involved in the relationship must engage in the work of rebuilding the relationship. Nevertheless, *the person who broke the trust must understand something. An open door of opportunity to repair the relationship is a gift from the other person and not to be taken lightly.*

Let's face it, it's an uncomfortable place to be, but as I have said before if you're the person who broke the trust—own up to it. Take responsibility for what was done, and you will take a giant step forward in helping to restore the relationship. What's more, if the other person has opened the door to you and given you the opportunity, if you are sincere, you must act now! This is no time to attempt to justify yourself or to wait for a better time. There is no better time than the present when given the opportunity to make amends.

Let me be clear, this "open door" should not be seen as a sign that all is well and back to normal and that the storm is about to blow over. It is an opportunity to rebuild. Fail to make the most of this opportunity and the storm will have just begun. Ignore or neglect this opening and it can destroy the relationship. That's right. Simply do nothing when the opportunity is presented and it can have devastating consequences. "But I never saw the person again," some would say. Or "I've changed. I am walking the 'straight and narrow' road now. I don't understand why we can't get past this."

A person cannot make amends to a relationship with another without involving the other. Those who try often do so because being open, honest, transparent, and accountable to the other person doesn't feel good after the betrayal. It reminds the person of something he would just as soon forget. One may feel as if he is "still being punished." The response is usually something like this, "It's over! It's in the past. Why can't we just move on?"

The question of "why" is the key to the whole situation. There is a reason. It is because betrayal is not something done alone and to oneself. We do not live in a void. We are connected to others and, as such, our work to rebuild a broken relationship will be unavoidably connected to others—especially the one whose trust we broke.

When we break the trust with another we can either chose to ease our guilty consciences or act to rebuild what we have broken. The difference in the two options is found in what we choose to do.

If all we want to do is ease our consciences we will justify ourselves at every turn, we will place just enough blame on the other person so as to cast ourselves in a better light, we might blame others, we might plead ignorance, or we might just try to pretend it didn't happen.

However, when we choose to rebuild or restore the broken trust our actions will reflect an entirely different mindset. The mindset behind these behaviors is something I want to discuss further. In a later chapter we will offer concrete examples of behavior when we revisit them.

Honesty

In most all cases, when there has been a trust broken, there has been a lack of honesty or outright deception. Once a person has been dishonest or deceptive there is much work to be done in restoring trust with others—especially with the one with whom you were dishonest. This is discouraging work at times because, as I have seen repeatedly in counseling sessions, even when the person is honest, he is doubted because of the events of the past. Many will say they just don't feel like they can win with those they failed. No matter how honest they may be, they are questioned as if they cannot be trusted ever again. The good news is that this will pass in most all cases, IF the necessary work is done. The less-than-good news is that the person who broke the trust must continue to live a consistently honest life in order to regain credibility. In other words, one must prove himself or herself.

At times it will be difficult to be questioned when there is no apparent reason for it, but endure anyway. One must do it for himself. He must want to be the kind of person of which he can be proud. It's not purely about pleasing another; it is about regaining what has been lost. What was lost, in part, was the sense of knowing one's mate could be trusted to not hurt him. Now the person who represented safety and security has become the source of hurt and pain. This has thrown the whole nature of the relationship off balance.

Dr. Donald Baucom from the University of North Carolina and Dr. Kristi Gordon from the University of Tennessee and authors of the book, *Getting Past the Affair,* and numerous scholarly articles on the subject of infidelity, explain in an article on "Treating Infidelity" what is taking place after the affair. "Following an affair, partners often lose predictability for their future and a loss of control, leading to deepened feelings of unbearable anxiety and despair." Suddenly everything is up in the air! Any appearance of control over their lives is gone. How do they know if anything is real anymore? One might think, *You say I can trust you from now on . . . I thought I could trust you before! How do I know now is different?* One can easily see how this could lead to despair.

Baucom and Gordon continue, "As long as injured partners don't have a clear understanding of why the affair or trauma occurred, they can't trust their participating partner not to hurt them again; instead, interactions with their partner may continue to trigger painful feelings." This is why honesty is so important in the rebuilding process. How can they move forward as long as there is too much uncertainty? It's not enough that you *know* you won't do it again—*she needs to know or feel* in some sense that you won't do it again, and that takes time for her to get to that place.

Honesty that is driven or motivated by fear of getting caught in a lie or simply out of practical necessity is a fragile honesty. The moment no penalty is possible or it serves no obvious purpose, is the moment it will fail. Honesty is certainly about being truthful and about having integrity, yet it is also about being reliable. Becoming a person who is reliable leads to one's being seen as dependable, consistent, and trustworthy. We cannot control others. We cannot always control circumstances; however, we have a considerable measure of control over ourselves. Thus, no matter what others do or say, we must remain consistent in our honest lifestyle to earn the trust of others.

Our honesty has to be motivated by something greater than other people's approval. One of the best ways of staying motivated is to develop an understanding of one's "internal locus of control." This is that inner sense of being able to control one's actions and affect the outcome of one's life. It is the understanding that we are responsible for our own success due to our decisions, choices, and attitudes. In a sense, it is the belief that we can change our destiny. This is even compatible with most views of the Christian faith, in that a person believes his prayers are an active work to change his life, and does not have to blindly accept whatever comes his way in life.

A person with an "external locus of control" usually believes his behavior and choices don't matter much—that what happens in life is generally out of his control. It is the sense that circumstances, misfortunes, fate, and even the decisions of others are responsible for the outcome of his life. People with this orientation are often fatalistic and say things like, "Whatever happens, happens" or "Que sera, sera" (Whatever will be, will be).

With an external locus of control, one will always be at the mercy of something or someone. One's feelings, mood, success, failure, attitude, happiness are all determined by those things outside his control. With an internal locus of control, one is empowered to choose, empowered to act, and has the ability to affect the outcome of one's life. Note that I said is "empowered" and not "can control." Control is a bit slippery. Just when you think it in your grasp, it slips away.

Being and feeling empowered at this point is essential because it can feel as if one is at the mercy of others due to past indiscretions. Additionally, one may find his honesty and sincerity accepted at times and questioned at times. It may be appreciated, but just as easily, it could be considered, "The least you could do." Either way, just remember, your decision to demonstrate your sincerity is yours alone. This decision is about who you have chosen to become.

Author and speaker, Dr. Kent M. Keith wrote,

> People are often unreasonable and self-centered. Forgive them anyway.
>
> If you are kind, people may accuse you of ulterior motives. Be kind anyway.
>
> If you are honest, people may cheat you. Be honest anyway.
>
> If you find happiness, people may be jealous. Be happy anyway.
>
> The good you do today may be forgotten tomorrow. Do good anyway.
>
> Give the world the best you have and it may never be enough. Give your best anyway.
>
> For you see, in the end, it is between you and God. It was never between you and them anyway.

Honesty is primarily between God and us. If no one but you and God know you are being sincere, keep going, others will be persuaded eventually, *if* you don't give up. We will speak more in a later chapter about practical actions and effective communication that convey honesty, but for now let's move on to openness and transparency.

Openness and Transparency

When trust has been broken in a relationship and deception has been laid aside, as we previously encouraged, the next step in restoring the relationship is a commitment to being open and transparent. It's almost the same as being honest, but for the sake of making a point, please permit me to split some hair and go a bit farther. A mindset of openness and transparency is fostered by the cooperative attitude of the person seeking to be open and transparent. The fact is our attitudes tend to leak out through our actions and one's goal can be thwarted by the lack of the right attitude. This is of great importance when we consider that openness and transparency is be defined as being "sincere, forthright, upfront, clear—not ambiguous." Well, I think that is clear. It shouldn't be hard to conform to such a clearly laid-out standard. Yet, unbelievably, it often is because of the person's attitude.

The reason conforming to this standard is frequently a problem is that some are being honest, but are not being clear or transparent. Some people have a habit of telling the truth while leaving the hearers in doubt they have just heard the truth. Clarity is a problem for them for one reason or another.

There may be other instances, but there are at least three when the lack of openness and transparency is a problem. First, consider a person who is trying to restore the trust she previously broke in her relationships. If, at some point, she *feels* she has something to hide to protect her from criticism, she may appear guarded or defensive. Regardless of whether or not there is a need for her to be concerned, if she feels the need to hide her behavior, conversations, intentions, or whatever, anyone who is the least bit suspicious of her will notice the diversions and secretive behavior. Again, she may be doing nothing wrong. She could just be concerned someone might accuse her; nevertheless, as long as her behavior and words appear secretive suspicion will be raised. Those closest to her who have been previously deceived will have a heightened awareness of her behavior. This is one reason the person who was found to have been deceptive, must realize, if caught in any *apparent deception* she will be accused quickly—even if there is no evidence of her guilt. The sensitivity of others will demand that openness and transparency become her new way of life.

Secondly, when a person is not rewarded for being open and transparent, but is instead penalized, it demotivates that person from trying to be transparent in the future. Some want to practice openness and transparency and will hide nothing, thinking they will be rewarded. Instead, the other party figuratively beats them to a pulp with their honesty. That's what happened with Bennie. She had dated a number of men prior to meeting and marrying Douglas. It wasn't that she was loose, but she was very attractive and got asked out a good bit. She lived in a very large metropolitan area. The supply of eligible bachelors was endless. She was single. She could date whomever she chose.

Prior to marriage Douglas knew she had been quite the socialite; however, after she and Douglas were married some of the men she had dated kept calling. They didn't know she had married and she would nicely explain and they would graciously apologize and not call back. It was annoying to Douglas at first, but then he found some text messages on her phone from men he didn't know. She was not at her office a few times she was supposed to be and could not be reached on her cell. In reality nothing was going on, but Douglas was convinced she was meeting up with one or more of those men. She would try to explain, but no explanation was good enough. She gave him access to her email account and her phone, invited him to drop by her office anytime, all to no avail.

Though he could prove nothing, he harassed her constantly about being honest with him. Nothing helped. Before she could ever speak in her own defense, she was being put on trial and convicted on every perceived infraction. Eventually she gave up and ceased to make those extra efforts to be open and transparent. She still told the truth, but the truth and nothing but the truth. There has to be an incentive for the person being open and transparent—if only peace and quiet.

Thirdly, when it is not clear to the person what constitutes openness and transparency, an explanation should be sought from the other person. I'm not prone to making excuses for people, but sometimes we need to seek greater understanding. One might think being open and transparent would be a familiar concept or at least easy to grasp. Sadly, I have actually seen some people whose family of origin was so dysfunctional that they find it difficult to function in what some might call a "normal" or functional family.

For example, imagine growing up in a home where illegal activities, drugs, alcohol abuse, and or conning or stealing was the norm. Now that person wants something better and finds a person from a healthy home—so much so, you'd think he was reared by Andy, Opie, and Aunt Bea in Mayberry. Do you really think both of these people are going to have the same understanding of what honesty, openness, and transparency mean? In the case he doesn't feel he is seeing open and transparent behavior, clarification must be given by the other person of exactly what is expected. Clarification without condemnation is the goal.

Clearly, openness and transparency is easier when one has done nothing wrong. Nevertheless, when a person has broken the trust of another there is the feeling of being the cause of a loss in the relationship. Now the other person wants him to expose even more of himself and his behavior. Already feeling defenseless, embarrassed, somewhat humbled, now more that feels the same is being demanded of them. No matter how much one feels he or she "has it coming" because of what was done, it is likely it is going to feel uncomfortable and even painful. Initially, the willingness to be open and transparent is a good start. You can build from there.

Accountability

To be accountable is to be answerable, yet this is not meant to be done in the sense one has to report to a parole officer or on the witness stand when one is on trial. Rather, accountability is an understanding one has a connection to another. Early on in counseling I am often looking for the right attitude to be manifested. I look for willingness by the person who broke the trust to be accountable to the other person. As with being open and transparent, accountability also may not equally be understood by both people. That can be taught. A willingness to be accountable—the right attitude—needs to be chosen.

The key with accountability is much the same with other aspects of rebuilding the connection in a relationship—give it time to work. Learning takes time. Change takes time. Personal growth takes time. Dr. Terry D. Hargrave reminds us, "Trustworthiness is a resource that accumulates over time to allow people to deal with each other based on realistic and valid assumptions and demonstrations of past reliability." Both will need time to process the hurt, the disappointment, the changes, learning to trust again, and more.

Concerning the time required in rebuilding accountability in the relationship, getting that connection back will be a hard-won victory. With that in mind, let me say with all consideration, it's not unfair—when we mess up and break the trust of another we must EARN that trust back. Now, as I have previously said and will say again, the betrayed person must be reasonable in his or her expectations, but being reasonable does not mean letting the person who broke the bond of trust set all the rules. That would be the equivalent of the old saying letting the fox be the one in charge of the hen house. Ideally, both people involved should sit down together and clarify expectations rather than one or the other setting all the expectations. If you're in counseling, this discussion should likely be included in one or more of your sessions.

For the person who broke the trust, it was people being unquestionably trusting and you deciding not to hold that trust sacred that got you into this place. The days of those same people being gullible are over. If that sacred trust is to be restored, it will be because you worked to restore it through responsible behavior. It will feel unfair at times and uncomfortable at times. Do it anyway. You may feel brought down a notch by communicating information about what you're doing or where you're going. Do it anyway. That is the way healthy relationships work and your attitude toward the process of rebuilding will be a critical factor.

Likewise, for the person who had her trust broken, the right attitude is of great importance. The quality of your attitude will either encourage the other person to remain engaged in the relationship or to give up trying to mend the relationship. Thus, demanding trust won't work. Punishing the other person for every perceived mistake won't work. Appearing to hold the other person in contempt will not help either. Attitude is important at this point.

In the next chapter we will look at some specifics of *how* one can prove oneself trustworthy and dependable.

Chapter Eleven

It's Time to Prove Yourself

· · · · · ·

If one wants to be a person who is trusted, one must live his or her life in a manner that inspires trust. For the person who has broken the trust of another, it may be a hard truth to reckon with, but that person must prove himself to the offended person. Hurt was inflicted and the original trust was ruined. The work of restoring the trust between them is the price of being seen as credible once again. In reality, all who are trustworthy live in such a manner that they prove themselves trustworthy every day. It is just that if anyone fails in this area, the proving of oneself has to start over. It can feel like being sent back to the starting line after one has run part of the race—frustrating—but that is the penalty.

One of the biggest complaints I hear from people trying to rebuild trust in their relationships is that the person who broke the trust hasn't yet, or isn't trying, to prove he can be trusted again. Usually this is not completely true. More often than not one of two things is happening. First, the person who has previously not shown herself trustworthy has made a genuine effort to be trustworthy, but the memory of her previous behavior is still too fresh in the mind of the person she hurt or others close to him. The second thing that is sometimes taking place is the person who was hurt has set his expectation level so high it leaves more room for disappointment than success for the person trying to do right. Consider a couple of possible scenarios:

Jill and Allen almost gave up and divorced after Jill's admission to an affair. Allen was devastated, but because he loved Jill so much he was willing to give her "another chance." Jill was relieved and sincerely wanted to prove herself and her love, and to work to save the marriage. As time passed over the next few months she was diligent in her efforts, always staying in communication with Allen when they were apart for long periods of time. She would even call during the day to tell him she loved him or to notify him of a change in her work schedule. Allen began to relax a bit and was beginning to feel Jill was truly committed to making the marriage work.

However, after about three or four months of this, Jill began to relax and felt the crisis was over and Allen trusted her once again. As a result, Jill made a few less calls during the week. Once again she was able to focus on her career and would allow herself to be consumed by her work. Time would pass. She would forget to call. The crisis was over now, and she didn't think it was a big deal. She started wanting to go out on Friday nights with her girlfriends again. She had been late coming home from work a few times and she had not called ahead of time to let Allen know there had been a change in her schedule. In reality, she was not doing anything wrong—hadn't even been tempted. Nevertheless, these little changes that resembled the "old Jill" unnerved him.

Then one of those nights Jill arrived home late without calling she found Allen sitting on the front steps waiting for her. By the time she reached the front door, Allen exploded! His slow-measured, angry tone quickly gave way to all-out shouting. "Where have you been?" He demanded to know.

"I was at work! Where do you think I was?" Jill responded.

Annoyed by her apparent lack of concern, Allen responds, "How am I supposed to know WHERE you are? You never called!"

Jill, angry herself by now, replies, "I told you I had a lot going at work this week. What? You think I was out with some other man?"

"Well," Allen counters, "what am I supposed to think?" (Watch out, here it comes), "You did it before, and how am I to know you're not doing it again!"

Jill tears up and begins to cry, "Are you never going to let me live that down?"

What has just taken place was hurtful and a mistake caused by an assumption. Allen handled the whole encounter wrong, but his fear had gotten the best of him. On the other hand, Jill made the mistake of going above and beyond in proving herself for the initial period after the affair, but fell back into what felt "normal" too quickly. She didn't realize the hurt was still too fresh in Allen's mind for the fear not to return. Plus, she had set the bar so high for her behavior by trying to quell Allen's fears that she couldn't sustain the pace. Thus, when she relaxed and took a more balanced approach, it looked suspicious in comparison.

Now, let's take the same couple and a similar situation. This time, imagine Jill going out of her way to be accountable and trustworthy with Allen as before. However, this time we see Allen continuing to raise the level of expectation. It looks something like this: No matter how many times she calls to check in, she "should have called" more. Even when she calls from work about a change of schedule, Allen doesn't believe her and will accuse her of lying and even drive by her office to make sure she is there. She is also no longer "permitted" to go out with her girlfriends unless he goes along too. If she says she is going to Wal-Mart, but comes home with a bag from Target, she is accused of being a liar and having met up with her supposed lover. The explanation that Wal-Mart was out of what she needed so she had to go down the street to Target is denounced as a lie to "cover her tracks."

At this rate, Jill feels she will never be able to prove herself. Yes, her infidelity started it all, but Allen says he wants the marriage to work. If nothing changes, Jill will likely give up trying and Allen will become embittered—all because they did not take a balanced approach to rebuilding trust in their relationship.

There Is More than Hurt

Anyone who has seen the trust in his or her relationship broken has faced a crisis that can threaten to consume his or her life. If those involved are not careful, the break will begin to characterize their lives, who they are and who they become, as well as the future decisions they make. To dwell on what has happened is to become cynical and hopeless. However, to make a home among the ashes of the failure is to deprive themselves of all the fulfilling and happy tomorrows they could have had together. Fatalism makes a person or a couple want to just sit down and give up. If you have failed or have a relationship that has experienced a failure, don't make a home among your failures. You were never meant to live there. This is not all there is.

"But they won't let me!" I hear people say. No one can stop you from doing what is right and helpful. The other person might not appreciate it at this point or may not feel it is enough, but you can do what you need to do to recover your dignity and your credibility. Some mistakes will be forgiven—all have to be outlived. Outlive your mistakes; don't allow them to define you. This chapter is about how to outlive your mistakes. I do not have a formula, or know of one, that will guarantee someone else will forgive you. That is out of our control. There is, however, a formula of sorts for regaining your credibility with yourself and with others.

Just as one's mindset must reflect a commitment, as I said previously, one's actions must also reflect a commitment in the three areas mentioned in the last chapter: first, honesty; secondly, openness and transparency; and thirdly, accountability. Again we will work to make a distinction in terms that essentially overlap in meaning.

Honesty

Telling the truth doesn't sound like a difficult task for most people, yet over the years, I have found it to be a great struggle for some. Although anyone can break another's trust, those who have a problem telling the truth will always be among those who break the trust of others. Obviously, people lie to get away with something or to avoid some kind of consequences, which is a problem no matter what the motive; still the bigger problem may be the feeling of some that lying is necessary or such a part of who they are, they do it without thinking.

It is such a problem that it is easy to find books, articles, blogs, and other sources of information on how to tell if someone is lying, types of lies, how to protect yourself from liars, and even how to tell better lies. The one subject few devote much time to writing about is how to tell the truth! The most reasonable explanation would be that people know how to tell the truth, they just find reasons for not doing it. This is the first topic on my list of ways to increase your honesty if being dishonest or lying is part of the reason you broke the trust in your relationship.

Don't Find a Reason to *Not* Tell the Truth

Being honest is easy until we anticipate conflict or some kind of negative consequence for our behavior. I understand the idea that if one has blown it in a relationship and the other person is already on edge that there would be a fear of saying too much or the wrong thing and making things worse. This is still not a good reason for *not* being honest. A lack of honesty erodes trust and at this point, you cannot afford to lose any ground in that area. Yes, it feels you're putting yourself at risk. You still must be honest.

Find *Your* Reason for Telling the Truth

Honesty that is demanded of a person becomes tiresome quickly. The same is true of trying to be honest because one feels guilty or because of peer pressure from family and friends. If a person doesn't want to demonstrate honesty for himself, because he sees the need and he wants to be a person of integrity, it won't work. Paying lip service to a life of honesty is hypocrisy at its best (or worst). Engaging in any pretense will only serve to destroy any potential gains in the relationship. This is not about fixing or making things better, or preventing someone from leaving or any other goal—except becoming the person you were expected to be in the beginning.

Balance Is the Key

This is what I have observed in instances where someone has broken the trust in the relationship. This is especially true with men. Men are "fixers." We don't know what we're doing half the time, but we're going to "fix it!" Some men will ask me, "How do I fix this?" The problem is often that they have already tried to "fix it" and have made it worse. I describe the usual behavior to the movement of a swinging pendulum. The behavior that caused the problem was the swinging of the pendulum to one extreme. The overcorrection by the person is the swinging of the pendulum to the other extreme.

It often happens something like this: Andrew had been using painkillers for a joyride. To be more specific, he had been eating Lortab, Lorcet, Oxycotin, and any other opiates he could find. He had successfully explained away the money disappearing, his loss of weight, his late-night runs to the store to get a few things, missing the children's soccer games—you get the picture. Then one day he got sloppy. His wife was putting away his socks and found a bottle in the drawer, hidden among the socks. She knew he had used drugs in the past, but that was before they were married. "He said he had quit!" she said to herself. She then looked them up on the Internet to make sure. She was right. She was furious!

I must have heard a variation of that story a hundred times. Different circumstances, different players, different consequences, different reactions, and far too often the person who messed up overcorrects. This brings us back to Andrew.

Andrew was a man who knew he had royally messed up! Not only was he married to a great woman, but he had three of the most darling children a man could imagine. In a strange way, he was glad he been caught. He was smart enough to realize he was using more than ever and that his money was running out. His lies and his tracks were getting hard to cover. This was going to be his turning point, he thought.

Gina, his wife, calmed down in a few days and told him she would stand by him while he got help and they would get through this together. He was so relieved he was willing to do anything to make her happy. In the following weeks he was the ideal husband, he was in counseling, and he was working on his recovery. He was more than accountable. He was too good to be true. That's a lot to ask of a man and for a man to ask of himself. Nevertheless, he was sincerely trying and that was a major step for him.

The problems began when he began to get tired and he began to relax. The crisis was over. He was doing everything he said he would do and it seemed all was well. The trouble was he had set the standard so high for himself he could not keep it up. Then his wife began to see him slipping from his lofty perch and began to question him and check up on him. At first, he was okay with meeting her expectations; after all, he messed up. Before long, however, her questions felt like interrogations, so he began to avoid her and react angrily when she brought things up. He felt persecuted and that he would never be good enough. Ironically, Andrew was beginning to rebel against the standard he had set for himself.

In this instance, Andrew's reaction was an overreaction to try to fix things. It could have been he wasn't sincere and was just trying to play the role of the perfect husband, thinking his wife would soon let the whole thing go and life could return to normal. When she didn't back off, he became angry at being held accountable. Even though that is a possibility, let's assume his heart was in the right place and he was just giving way to his manly instincts to try and fix things. Whatever the case, he offered too much and went too far. The pendulum had swung too far to the other extreme. The result was Andrew began to be resentful toward his wife and realized he couldn't live up to the standard he had set for himself. The outcome was he and Gina were farther apart than before.

Several mistakes were made. First, Andrew decided on his new standard of behavior without discussing it with Gina. She may have had a more level-headed approach. He never asked. Secondly, *he went into fix-it mode instead of into relationship-building mode.* The relationship becoming stronger would have helped repair much of the problem. Andrew once again went it alone. Thirdly, he saw himself as his greatest resource and depended only on himself. He failed to realize his wife could have been a great source of strength. This is common among people with addictions. Fourthly, communication was almost non-existent throughout the whole ordeal. I'm sure you may see other mistakes, and what I encourage you to do is to examine your situation, think it through, see your mistakes, and work with the other person in the relationship to set reasonable, shared goals and expectations. See one another as a source of strength and support, and balance can be achieved.

Openness and Transparency

It is much easier to be genuine, accountable, and honest in a relationship when one has nothing to hide. As I have indicated before, some people have the ability or practice the technique of telling the truth while leaving out details. Then is that truly the truth? No, it is probably not the truth if the person is *intentionally* leaving out details. When this is done, at least two problems can arise. First, the person who has broken the trust of another could decide to continue to withhold information from the other person with the intention of preventing further harm. Secondly, the person who was wronged will refuse to believe he has the whole story, no matter how much information is freely given. As one might expect, one problem can feed off or create the other problem.

It works this way. If I ever catch you withholding information from me, I may have difficulty believing you are telling me the whole story in the future. It will not matter what your reason might have been. Likewise, if you never believe me, no matter how much I spill my guts to you, my motivation for disclosing information to you will likely decrease. I'm getting penalized no matter what I do. Wisdom and restraint is called for on the part of both. The person who has been deceptive must work to eliminate all deception; however, the offended person must realize transparency has limitations in that the other person will not always know what is expected as far as details unless it is made clear. Additionally, discretion can still be a good thing. I have seen people push, push, and push for every conceivable detail and, once receiving them, wish they had not pushed so hard. The key here is relevance—is it important to the ability to trust? Some would say, "Yes!" I need to know everything going through his mind!" To which I would say it is likely either your anxiety is out of control and/or you have issues with controlling others.

Transparency demands we keep things simple. Eliminate all ambiguity or vagueness from your explanations, whereabouts, associations, and plans. There can't be unexplained or unexplainable events, calls, relationships, or appointments. "I don't like being treated like a child!" some protest. Usually the proper response would be, "Stop acting like a child." People feel the need to parent us, yes, because they have issues, but also because we often fall into the role of a child in our behavior.

People seem to want to control others either because they feel they deserve to or because their anxiety level is so high when they are not controlling something or somebody. My father was the latter. Anxiety often drove his behavior. He would go into controlling mode when he was unnerved or worried. I remember an incident like that. This was before the age of cell phones or even pagers—yes, I'm evidently ancient—and he wanted to know where his kids were all the time. Good dad. He should have wanted that, but for a teen boy, being tracked down by your freaked-out dad late at night because he didn't know if I "was in a ditch somewhere, dead!" was not a good experience.

As a result, I learned quickly to eliminate Dad from going into control mode, I needed to behave as an adult. As long as I called and let him know where I was and what I was doing, he was fine. Simple consideration eliminated the problem. Later in life, I suppose because he was uneasy about everything turning out good for me, so he wanted to decide my profession, where I lived, and several other decisions. That is where I drew the line. Sometimes controlling to reduce anxiety is understandable; sometimes it is crossing the line. Being relentless with your offender to the point he feels constantly under interrogation is crossing the line.

Some behaviors stick with us for a lifetime. All these years later, after thirty years of marriage, I still call every afternoon on my way home from work and say, "I'm on my way home. Do you need me to pick up anything?" And yes, I would track my daughters down in a New York minute if I didn't know where they were, but I choose not to try to plan their lives. The bottom line for anyone who has faltered in the area of trust is that there are countless little ways we can be open and transparent, removing all doubt or uncertainty, about who we are and what we're doing and whether or not we can be trusted. The solution is found in the old Nike advertisement: "Just do it!" Hopefully you will receive grace from the other person.

The Basics of Rebuilding Trust through Transparency

The following are a few of those ways we can work toward rebuilding trust with another through being open and transparent:

- Break all contacts with those involved with your previous breach of trust. For example: any and all persons involved in one's infidelity, drug use, gossip, backstabbing, or dishonest financial dealings.

- Continue to accept full responsibility for one's behavior. Constantly seeking to justify one's previous behavior will only lead to doubt of your sincerity being cast in the mind of those betrayed.
- Take the initiative in creating a new "normal" for the relationship in which trust will be easier to reestablish. If you know what the other person needs to feel he/she can trust you—take action.
- Be willing to continue to answer the questions the betrayed person may have and make it easy for her to ask the questions by being open and not giving a defensive or angry response.
- Don't expect the other person to just "get over it." That would appear to minimize the offense. One's acceptance of the other person's pain validates and affirms the other person.
- Talk, communicate, and interact with the betrayed person. Withdrawing or being silent only adds to his suspicion.

Accountability

The failure to be accountable and be trustworthy hurts more than the relationship between two people. It usually hurts all the relationships connected to that relationship as well. In addition to a spouse knowing she can trust you, children need to know they can trust their parents. This is hugely important. Family members, in-laws, one's own parents, and friends become concerned and sometimes doubtful of a person when there is a refusal on someone's part to be accountable. This is why accountability is so important. It is about more than accepting responsibility for oneself and one's actions; it is about one's integrity and trustworthiness; it is the understanding of one's connectedness with those around him, that no one lives totally to himself, and what he chooses to do or to be has an impact on others.

After the trust in a relationship is broken, even when there is a desire on the part of the individual who broke the trust to be accountable, the faith of others in that person is often restored more slowly than the person hoped. If that is your dilemma, let me encourage you not to give up if trust isn't restored quickly. Frequently I see people who just want to say they are "sorry" and everything go back to the way it was—sorry, it's just not going to happen. Love doesn't give free passes nor does love ask for a free pass. If you have broken someone's trust in a serious manner, understand this, she has been hurt. Look at it this way, she has been injured emotionally and needs time to recover. Trust can be destroyed quickly, but it is rarely built quickly.

Accountability Is Your Choice

As previously noted, accountability that is demanded or required will usually lead to resentment and resistance. The way around this obstacle is found in being proactive. Don't wait for accountability to be discussed by the other person, open the conversation yourself. Let him know you want to prove yourself and you have no problem being accountable. One way I suggest to individuals they can do this, with men especially, is that they consider offering their accountability to the other persons who have reason to question them, as a gift. It's about exercising choice. It's about making it an act of love. It's about setting the tone. Ribbons and wrapping paper are not required—a benevolent heart is required.

This "gift" as I call it is the proactive or practical decision to make better choices, life changes, and behavior changes. For instance, a person with a history of a previous drug addiction, affair, gambling problem, etc. must accept that some behaviors are no longer acceptable. *These behaviors include, but are not limited to the following:*

- Having an additional cell phone you keep hidden, numerous calls to or from the same unknown number,
- Unexplainable expenses showing up on the credit card or checking account,
- The need to always have a large amount of cash on you,
- Going out alone unexpectedly or late at night with no explanation that makes sense to the other person,
- Unexplained absences from home or work, and like behaviors

Like it or not, these are all real reasons for others to distrust you.

Additionally, teenagers who have a history of slipping out of the house, skipping school, getting in trouble with drugs, lying, surfing porn, hanging out with others your parents have forbidden, staying out beyond curfew, coming home high or intoxicated, etc., you have hurt your reputation or the way people see you. You could yell, scream, accuse the world and your parents of being "unfair", and insist you are misunderstood. All that does about as much good as banging your head against the wall—which by the way, you should *not* do. It causes "drian bramage."

Seriously, if the previous explanation describes you or your teen, and the teen in question has a desire to be accountable and earn back her good name, the new reality will have to be something like this: No more locking herself away in her room, refusing to open the door. She must begin allowing her surfing history on the Internet to be checked. She must tell the truth, realize how her behavior affects the family and others' impression of her character. Additionally, you will need to realize she has no business staying out later than the set curfew, being secretive, hanging out with people she knows have a bad reputation, hiding things, even appearing high or intoxicated and so forth.

No matter who we are, becoming enraged when we're questioned only hurts our argument that we're innocent or being cooperative. In addition, being evasive and not giving a straight answer is a red flag. You understand. The only solution is accountability. In most cases, the trust in your relationship can be restored. It's time to prove yourself and with a genuine effort, you can do it.

CHAPTER TWELVE

Tough Questions Remain

······

When I began writing on the question of how trust is restored I had no intention of writing a book on the subject. Additionally, the more research I did on the topic the more I became convinced it would be difficult to concisely address all the questions, either asked of me in the past or raised by the discussion; nevertheless, here we are, trying to answer all the questions we can in one text. The following are numerous questions that may not have smoothly fit into the other chapters, yet I wanted to attempt to give an answer. So, let us begin.

Q. Is it wrong to want the person who broke your trust to "prove" themselves?

A. No. However, the question is "how" are they going to prove themselves? What are your demands? A big mistake would be to set the standard too high. Do this and you will kill the other person's motivation to prove himself. No matter how sincere a person is in setting things right, a person has his limits.

Also, ask yourself if you really want him to pay for what he did. Expecting penance, a show of humility or sorrow can be tricky.

Depending on a person's personality, gender, and more these feelings will be expressed differently. In fact, if a person was taught by a parent that tears and words mean little and actions speaker louder, don't expect that person to tearfully apologize. It's more likely he will try to do something to show he is remorseful. Likewise, the opposite is true. For some, a tearful apology was always enough. Now you are expecting them to do something. Be clear what you are looking for and work with the person's true nature.

Q. When there is a multitude of transgressions, am I encouraging them to do it again by forgiving them?

A. It depends on how the forgiveness is offered. How we approach this will indeed have an effect on how we will be treated in the future. If it is offered in a way that frees the other person or persons of all responsibility and guilt of what they did, then it could leave the door open for it to happen again. We must constantly conduct ourselves in a manner that teaches others how we want to be treated. Consequently, when the responsibility of what they have done continues to be an important part of the equation—not continually thrown up in their face—but understood as central to the apology and assumed mending of the relationship, then we are not doing something that will only present another open opportunity for them to repeat the wrong.

The key is to be clear, fair, and balanced in our response to anyone who has broken our trust—especially when it is clearly a matter of intentional deceit.

1. Be clear about what has been done. Be clear about how you feel and what you feel it means to the relationship.
2. Be fair and willing to at least consider that the breach in trust was not a premeditated act. Many people are impulsive

and genuinely regret their behaviors afterward. Give them a reasonable way to make things right.

3. Be balanced in your response. Nothing hinders a person's desire to make amends and apologize like the other person "going off on them" as some would say—in other words, getting hysterical, emotionally outraged, and going on the attack. If you have to, wait until you can be calm and balanced in your conversation.

Q. Is there something wrong with them mentally for them to have done this?

A. I often hear people playing armchair psychiatrist when they have been lied to, deceived, cheated on, or hurt repeatedly by the same people. Some have said, "I think" or "My friend said they must be a sociopath!" Or the ever-popular, "They're bi-polar!" Those who have been hurt, as well as their family and friends, often "diagnose" people who have hurt them as being "mental" or "sick." I think it somehow makes them feel better if they can come up with a reason for those persons' behavior other than to feel that they just disrespected them.

While it is possible, some people who continually break the trust between themselves and others may be emotionally unwell or even have a full-blown personality disorder, we should still be careful not to demonize the other person too quickly or play armchair psychiatrist. I say this for a few reasons.

First, they *may not* have a diagnosable mental condition or personality disorder (only a qualified professional can diagnose) and labeling them as though they do will only push them away. Secondly, labeling the offending person frees us too quickly from our responsibility in the relationship. For example, when a person labels the one who broke her trust as "mental" or in some other way, instantly she is setting herself up to feel that she is not responsible for working on the relationship because the other person is somehow broken.

Let's face it, if the first time a person questions another's state of mind is when he breaks his trust, it is likely the person in question is probably not mentally unhinged. People with real personality disorders and diagnosable mental illnesses usually get people's attention a little earlier on in the relationship. Don't fall into the trap of labeling the person to justify your decisions or feelings. If you do not like the way a person is treating you, then you have every right to speak up and hold her accountable for her behavior. If you continue to have concerns about someone, take her, or refer her to a qualified professional for personality testing and counseling.

Finally, the truth of the matter is some people have a habit of lying to avoid punishment or penalties of some kind. Others fail others because a sense of character and integrity was not instilled in them early in their lives. Some are just selfish and self-centered and no one has really ever challenged them. Lastly, some people are impulsive and act before they think things through. Always try boundaries and accountability first; if this doesn't work seek out a qualified professional to help with your relationship.

Q. When can I start believing them again?

A. You can begin anytime you choose and to whatever degree you choose. The better question to begin with might be, "How much *what?* faith am I willing to put in a flawed human being?" Defining expectations here is important. What are your standards? "Well, I have high standards, but no higher than I have for myself!" Perhaps a little adjustment to the standard might be in order in some cases, depending on your personality and perspective. For example, you may have read about or taken one of the personality profiles that divide personalities into four basic types. Most all people are a blend of the four, while some are much more of a thoroughbred of one type. Case in point, some have a personality type focused on rules, order, and details, and they see matters of right and wrong in black-or-white terms. There are other people with a personality type that is primarily relational and focus on feelings and emotions. They see matters of right and wrong in shades of gray.

If I had the first type of personality I would have zero patience with people who didn't get it right or do it right. I would see that person as undisciplined and undependable. If I had the second type of personality, I would be flexible and easy-going, more concerned with hurting your feelings than making you follow the rules, and I would see the other personality type as controlling and critical. Neither personality would make me a better person, but would influence my behavior. The better place to be, in this example, is a blend of the two.

My point is that rarely do others live up to being the same as we see ourselves. Grace is the operative term here. They probably do not have the same background or life experiences as you. What was their family like? What values were instilled in them? What forces have shaped them? When possible and advisable, extend a little underserved grace to the other person and encourage them to become what *they* can become.

Oswald Chambers wrote, "Jesus Christ never trusted human nature, yet he was never cynical, never in despair about any man, because he trusted absolutely in what the grace of God could do in human nature." Accepting people as they are and then clearly setting our personal boundaries and non-negotiable expectations early on will often serve us better than demanding they measure up to our personal standards after they have failed us in some way.

The bottom line: Understand what is at stake. If having the person in question fail you *again* would result in catastrophic consequences for you or others, you must weigh your options carefully. It is one thing to trust that someone with a sketchy character is going to repay you the fifty dollars he borrowed, it's quite another to trust the same person with your entire retirement savings. The question is, can you bear the failure should it happen?

Q. Where do I draw the line?

A. With repeat offenders there's always that proverbial "straw" that threatens to break the camel's back—that one thing that pushes you too far. Strangely it may be something that is minor in comparison to the previous offenses, but it was one too many! For the person who has repeatedly crossed the line, a sudden enforcement of your limit will seem odd to her. After all, you and I may have set a precedent of overlooking and forgiving that has left her with the idea she could continue doing what she has always done. I believe we teach people how to treat us and sometimes we teach them the wrong thing. We inadvertently teach them they can treat us as they choose without any real repercussions. Our "line" means nothing to them. At this point, we must draw a new line. "But where?" many ask.

The line is drawn where safety ends and harm begins. There are some instances where a person attempting to trust someone could place herself in danger of physical harm, emotional harm—to herself or others—financial ruin, and even legal troubles. This is never advised. If this is the case, clear boundaries should be in place. While you can assure the person you care for him and want the best for him, you must also let him know what your limits are in regards to what you can and will do. Prepare to be accused of being unfair, of not truly forgiving him, of not loving him, or to be engaged in an argument designed to wear you down. Don't budge. If the other person is truly sorry and willing to accept the responsibility for what he has done in the past, he may not like it, but he will have to respect your limitations.

It would seem we humans have a limit to how much we can get beyond emotionally and thus we are often looking for a way out of the cycle of hurt. In Matthew 18:21-23 of the New Testament, Jesus was asked, "Lord, how many times shall I forgive my brother who sins against me? Up to seven times?" Jesus answered, "I tell you, not seven times, but seventy [times] seven times" (NIV).

No, he is not saying four-hundred-ninety times. He is making the point that there is no limit to how much we forgive. "That's outrageous!" some who are looking for justice might complain. Surely, there has to be a balance, we can't just allow others to transgress against us without there being a limit? There is a balance; however, it is not found in withholding forgiveness from someone who asks for it. Nor is the balance found in the number of times we forgive verses the number of times they ask. The balance is found in our ability to forgive and set good boundaries.

Always remember, *the only person you can control is you!* There is no way you can control the other person or what she can do—at least not legally. What you do in response to what others say and do is all you can control. Forgiveness is what you *can* control and ultimately, forgiveness benefits you more than anyone. The encouragement to forgive as many times as you're asked is meant to keep you free—free from bitterness, hatred, spite, and anger which all serve to rob you of an enjoyable life. Unforgiving people go on with their lives all the time with apparent ease. It is unusual to hear someone all torn up emotionally years later because someone didn't forgive them. Just the same, it is extremely common to meet people seething with bitterness years later because they did not forgive.

So, is that all? No. *While forgiveness will set us free, good boundaries keep us safe.* This is where drawing a line comes into play. We don't draw the line at how many times we forgive; we draw the line at how much access we will allow the other person to have into our lives. Many mistakenly think if they forgive someone, everything should go back to exactly the way it was before the wrongdoing or else they have not truly forgiven. Not so! That is a common misunderstanding.

Imagine a person you thought was your friend has been gossiping about what you told her in private and even telling lies about you, possibly damaging your relationship. You confront her. She tearfully apologizes and gives a feeble, but seemingly sincere, apology explaining that she got caught up in trying to be accepted by another group of people you both know. You forgive and with time, it seems all is well again. That is until you find out she did it again! To make matters worse, this happens a few more times. Then, it finally appears the person has ruined her own reputation, been rejected by others, and has learned her lesson. She apologizes— again. Do you forgive her? Yes. Do you treat her well when you're around her? Yes. Do you still try to love her? Yes. Do you let her back into your life in the same kind of relationship you had originally? NO! It can be a friendly, caring relationship, but you would not do well to give her unlimited access to your life.

Q. What if it has *ALL* just been one big lie?

A. I will admit that some I have known who continually break the trust of others can themselves appear to forget what is real and what is not. Some lie when there is a reason and even when there is no reason whatsoever to lie. A few devote an inordinate amount of time trying to make the other person feel he is the center of his universe only to abandon him once the charade has been believed. These are manipulators of the highest order.

If this is the type of person with which you are contending, I would again recommend reading the book, *Safe People*, and add to that the book, *Emotional Vampires: Dealing with People Who Drain You Dry,* by Dr. Al Bernstein and get them in professional counseling if possible.

That said, allowing oneself to fixate on it ALL being "one big lie" can be emotionally unhealthy for the person on the receiving end of the apparent deception. This line of thinking leads us to what has been called "catastrophizing," exaggerating the implications, or blowing things out of proportion. Ironically, it is a thought pattern not based in truthfulness. Again, we are assuming the person you're dealing with, or thinking about, is not a sociopath. If that was the case, some things were likely not a lie. In fact, the truth mixed in with the lies is what makes it even more confusing.

Why you should guard against this line of thinking is simple: it is apt to cause cynicism in future relationships with people who *can* be trusted. I have seen it many times. After a failed relationship someone finally finds a good, decent, honest person with whom to have a relationship and she drives the person away with her total lack of trust. Then the person feels foolish having realized what she has done and feels worse about herself. It can become a dysfunctional cycle and the cycle produces cynicism and fatalistic thinking. Next, the person feels, "There's no use in trying."

Q. What do we do when the trust has been broken so many times?
A. Choosing to be in relationship with someone who has repeatedly broken trust is not going to be easy. It will take time for him to prove himself to you and time for you to get beyond the hurt. Mark Twain had a saying about learning from our mistakes, "We should be careful to get out of an experience only the wisdom that is in it—and stop there, lest we be like the cat that

sits down on a hot stove-lid. She will never sit down on a hot stove-lid again—and that is well; but also she will never sit down on a cold one anymore." Put another way, don't allow yourself to be burned so many times you avoid all relationships. Learn from your experiences whatever lesson is there and respond using that wisdom. A better question for this person might be, *"Why have you allowed yourself to be treated this way for so long?*

Q. If I tell them I forgive them, does that mean I can never talk about it again?

A. Talking about it and holding it over a person's head are two different things. An example: A guy complained to his buddy that whenever he argued with his wife, she got historical. His friend said, "You mean hysterical." He said, "No, historical. She digs up my past mistakes and reminds me of every time I've ever failed her." If the memory of the breach of trust becomes a stick to beat the other over the head with, then don't talk about it anymore.

Additionally, if the past failure becomes a way of never allowing the other person to feel good about himself again, then leave it alone. This usually takes place something like this: the person who broke the trust or failed in some way tries to point out the progress she has made or the changes she has made for the better. In some way, she is casting herself in a positive light. Then it happens. The person who was "done wrong" starts up. It's called "motor boating" and it goes something like this: But, but, but, but . . . *(Sounds like a motor boat engine—laugh here).* To more clearly explain, the response sounds like this, "Yes, you're doing better, but . . ." or "I know what I said hurt your feelings, but . . ." In other words, the person who erred will never get the chance to feel good about herself in the presence of the other.

Nevertheless, bringing something up one has learned from previous experience, in a positive way, can be an acceptable way to talk about something in the past. Listen for insights gained, affirmations, understanding, talk of progress, etc., if these are missing, end the conversation.

Q. What if they just won't admit to their wrongdoing?

A. In some instances a few individuals will often act and talk as if they want the broken relationship to be whole again, except they will never actually admit to having done anything wrong. Sometimes they will dance around the issue with vague language and offer half-way apologies mixed with a good bit of blaming others. At times, as we mentioned in an earlier chapter, they might even admit they did do or say something wrong, but they will excuse themselves by saying that they only did or said what is in question *because* of what someone else did or said to them. Thus, they never really admit to actually being in the wrong themselves. Last of all, there are those who will refuse to admit they did wrong under any circumstances!

Bottom line: No admission of wrongdoing, when wrong has obviously been done, lets us know the person takes no responsibility for his or her behavior and is most likely an "unsafe" person.

Q. What if I have apologized repeatedly and the other person won't truly forgive me, but neither will she let me go?

A. There are instances in which a person who has been wronged in a relationship uses the infraction of the other person to give her the upper hand in the relationship. The fact the person "failed her" becomes something she can use to exercise power over the offender. To forgive would be to relinquish this new power. There might be a struggle or a resistance to giving up that so-called power because just bringing up the hurt—what was done—will often result in the offender giving in to the wishes of the person she hurts. It is a "trump card" or an "ace up their sleeve" so to speak. Anytime she is not winning, the person can play that card and win.

First, one would need to make sure the person who has been hurt is not genuinely struggling with the hurt. Don't naturally assume if forgiveness does not occur within a certain time frame that the other person is manipulating you. Forgiveness often takes longer than feels comfortable for the person seeking forgiveness. Nevertheless, if you feel you are being manipulated with the memory of your past wrong so the other person can have his way, it's likely you have encountered an "emotional vampire." This is one type of person you *do not* want to fail. I refer you once again to Dr. Al Bernstein's best seller, *Emotional Vampires*.

In his book, Bernstein repeatedly points out that emotional vampires find life to be a lonely experience. Thus, "For them, the world comprises only their needs, nothing else." Of course, these are not just the run-of-the-mill needy people. He explains, "Emotional vampires are people with personality disorders," explaining, "when people are driving themselves crazy, they have neuroses or psychoses. When they drive other people crazy, they have personality disorders." They are easy to spot because they often want to control everything and everyone—because they know best of course. When upset or under stress, they behave like "emotional two-year-olds." Just don't expect them to see their childish ways for what they are. He clarifies the "basic social rules" of emotional vampires as being: "My needs are more important than yours; the rules apply to other people, not me; it's not my fault, ever; I want it now; if I don't get my way, I throw a tantrum."

You're probably getting the picture already. Others, you in this case, are responsible for their happiness, consequently, it is only natural to control you, manipulate you, get you to give in, back down, stay in your place, and otherwise adapt to their wants and wishes and needs so they can be happy.

One note of caution here: Make *sure you are not* the emotional vampire wanting someone else to cease his holding you accountable because it makes you unhappy. Reading Dr. Bernstein's book can help, but you might also want to get honest feedback from others you trust. A professional counselor can also help guide you through achieving greater self-awareness. Just *don't* ask the person from whom you are seeking forgiveness. That person will almost certainly accuse you of being an emotional vampire—especially if he is a "vampire" himself!

Q. Can my relationship survive the broken trust of infidelity?

A. Not to be vague or uncommitted, it depends. Yes. It is possible. No. No one has a guaranteed formula to work every time, no matter what. While there are successful formulas, so much is beyond the control of any one person. Allow me to quote an expert in the field, Adrian J. Blow, PhD, in his work on helping couples move through the pain of infidelity. He writes, "More than likely the best answer to this question is, it depends, on variables such as the type of infidelity, duration of the problem, values of the clients, other difficulties in the relationship, and most importantly, commitment of both parties to change."

The bad news is when the infidelity remains secret and unaddressed; the threat to the marriage is tremendous. However, the good news is for couples who are honest with one another and proactive in their approach to addressing the infidelity, they can and do recover from infidelity and go on to have long and happy marriages.

I hope that we were successful here in filling in some of the gaps in the information presented. Now, let's move on to the final chapters where we hope to complete our reconstruction of relational trust.

Chapter Thirteen

What Does a Healthy, Trusting Relationship Look Like?

· · · · · ·

Whether it's a marriage or a friendship or a family relationship, healthy relationships have several common components such as: the people involved care for one another, are respectful to and of one another and their boundaries, depend on one another without apprehension—in other words they're comforting and nurturing. People in healthy relationships don't try to make the other person(s) responsible for their happiness or their failures. A healthy relationship is based on love—real love—not the movie kind or the idealized "soul mate" kind, or the "I feel loved if I get my own way" kind.

You have probably heard about this "real love" at almost every wedding you've attended. It's when the minister reads 1 Corinthians 13, verses four through seven. As you read what it says, stop and think about what it says. It's not for newlyweds. It is for human beings in all types of relationships. The apostle Paul enlightens us, "Love is patient and kind. Love is not jealous or boastful or proud or rude. It does not demand its own way. It is not irritable, and it keeps no record of being wronged. It does not rejoice about injustice but rejoices whenever the truth wins out. Love never gives up, never loses faith, is always hopeful, and endures through every circumstance" (NLT).

Take a moment and absorb the truth about love. Without an understanding of the truth about love and a commitment to it, a healthy, trusting relationship is not possible. All of the aspects of love described in 1 Corinthians are the aspects of love anywhere one goes, any time in which one lives, any circumstance one faces, with anyone with whom you have a relationship. Do you want a picture of a healthy relationship in which trust can grow? There it is.

Of course, I realize some people who may have never known what it means to be in a healthy, trusting relationship may need more examples of how that kind of love would play out in their lives. It may feel for some as if everyone they have ever tried to get close to ended up hurting them, deceiving them, or letting them down in a significant manner. Consequently, if that is a person's frame of reference for a relationship, the idea of building a healthy, trusting relationship may seem an unfamiliar concept. Rather than leave people wondering about what constitutes a good relationship and how one might go about developing one, I have found over the years that it can be helpful to "paint a picture," so to speak, of what I have in mind. From that point, each person can adjust the mental image to fit one's life and needs. With that in mind, consider the following examples of what a trustworthy person and relationship might look like. Note how they compare with the apostle Paul's words. Keep in mind, participation of all parties involved is required for a relationship to work, no matter how much love *you* have in your heart.

Let's begin painting our picture of a healthy relationship with a look at the family—where it all begins. Then we will move on to other types of relationships, and of course, the marriage relationship.

Healthy Families

The reason it is important to understand the components of a healthy family is so that there is a frame of reference for what is healthy and emotionally safe within the scope of these relationships. As I often tell people, whatever you grew up in was "normal" for you, no matter how much you hated it or wanted something different, and without a plan to be different, we gravitate toward what is normal for us. This is a big problem when "normal" has always been a bad thing. If the norm for your childhood household was good, that's great, you are fortunate. You most likely have a good idea of what I mean when I speak of a healthy, trusting relationship. Unfortunately, many do not have that same understanding. The good news for those who have never known a good normal when it comes to relationships is that you can learn to create a new normal for yourself that is good. You are not powerless—just prone to be like those we know best—our family of origin.

Ever wonder why we unconsciously do the things we do sometimes or sound like our parents? *(Please be aware this is somewhat of an oversimplified explanation.)* It's what we know best. Have you ever been upset that you yelled, screamed, or were critical of your children just as your parents did to you? It's what you know from your experience. That kind of behavior was "normal" for your home when you were a child. For people who grew up in a home in a constant uproar, where yelling and hitting and cursing was the norm, had they been plucked out of that home and moved to a home down the street where none of that took place and people were kind, gentle, and had normal conversations, the person would have likely felt uncomfortable. She may have loved it; however, it would not have felt natural. If you have never known an emotionally healthy home, your challenge is to build one so that trust can have a place to grow.

Rather than just sharing my opinion or observations on this I want to draw from authorities in the study of relationships. Although healthy families have numerous strengths, some appear to have a greater influence on the outcome of child rearing. In an article called, "Family strengths: Often overlooked, but real," researchers found a connection between certain strengths in families and the well-being of the children. Those strengths were found to be:

1. *Positive mental health in parents*

   Children whose parents say that they feel calm, peaceful, or happy are more likely than other children to be positively involved in school and less likely to act out or have emotional problems.

2. *Everyday routines*

   Families that tend to have regular routines and roles usually have children who do well in school and have greater self-control. Keeping these everyday routines (like eating together and doing household tasks) is associated with positive outcomes for adolescents. They are more likely to avoid delinquent behavior and less likely to use drugs.

3. *Spending time together*

   Having fun with one's family is related to better outcomes for adolescents. Again, adolescents are more likely to avoid delinquent behavior and less likely to use drugs. Quality time is important for happiness in family relationships.

4. *Communication and praise*

   Positive communication (being warm, respectful, and interested in a child's opinions) is associated with the well-being of children. Two-way communication can encourage healthy behavior in adolescents. Adolescents who have parents that use praise and who go to their parents for advice are less likely to have behavioral and emotional problems.

5. *Monitoring, supervision, and involvement*
   When parents use praise and encouragement, show awareness, and monitor adolescents' schoolwork and social life, their children tend to do better in school and show more socially positive behaviors.

Strengths related to family relationships:

6. *Warm and supportive relationships between the parent and child*
   Warm and supportive relationships with parents are associated with good adolescent outcomes. Adolescents with these types of relationships are less likely to be suspended from school, are less likely to have behavioral and emotional problems, and are less likely to abuse substances.

Children want to feel closely connected to the members of their family, they want to feel loved, and that they are an important part of the lives of the others in the family. Consequently, when one feels disconnected, unappreciated, unvalued, constantly blamed or criticized, it is only natural to expect unhealthy behavior such as lying and deceptive behavior that leads to a lack of trust with that member of the family. Labeling the child as a "bad seed" is unproductive and shows an unwillingness to see and address the deeper issues in the family.

Healthy Parenting

Everyone seems to know how to be an expert parent—except people with children. You know the ones, those with *imaginary* children, who have never had any. But for those who are *parents of real*, lovely, sweet, smart, awesome, yet aggravating, whiney children who cause us to stop in our tracks and wonder, "What were they thinking?" and if we're going to lose our minds—*we* have questions. *We* have struggles. *We* know answers aren't easy to find at times. *We* blow it at times. *We* have doubts of whether or not we're doing a great job. Consequently, let's put aside the idea there are perfect families and perfect children and perfect parents here and now! They don't exist. This doesn't mean, however, we can't improve. Consider a few ways we might be able to improve:

First, as a rule, parents should guard against negative feelings between themselves affecting their children whether as a part of a disagreement over a parenting or home life decision or more serious issues. Many couples become more aware of this rule if they are obviously having problems or are involved in a marriage separation or divorce. They may try to shield the children. Unfortunately, some use their children as allies, pawns, messengers, shields, or as scapegoats whether in divorce or not. My point is simple: if it can be prevented at all, the children should not suffer from the spillover of emotions, anger, hurt, betrayals, or similar actions. If not prevented, this can happen in obvious ways. Some examples would be that of parents pulling their child into an argument to side with one or the other, or by lashing out at the child or children when really angry with the other parent. Parents need to be careful not to depend on a child for emotional support or to act as a confidant on a regular basis as would an adult. What is not always considered is that according to an article in the *American Journal of Family Therapy*, on the subject of "Training Parents in Forgiving and Reconciling," the authors conclude,

> High stress is positively correlated with low parental warmth, reciprocity, unhealthy parenting styles, harsh discipline, and even abuse and/or neglect. Similarly, parental conflict is associated with a number of adverse outcomes of childhood development and adjustment— such as detriments to emotional regulation, attachment, social skill development, self-efficacy, and triangulation. Thus, chronic levels of unforgiveness, which exacerbate parental stress and conflict, may contribute to inconsistent, unsupportive, or even abusive behavior by parents and result in detriments to the children's development. In addition, the parent's inability to handle conflict effectively may lead to unhealthy relationship dynamics between parent and child.

As we can see, a home life where hostility, criticism, unforgiveness, a lack of emotional warmth, harsh discipline, and so forth are modeled, the development and understanding of healthy, trusting relationships are undermined. In light of this, it is easy to conclude that working toward maintaining and/or developing healthy relationships, even in terms of parenting, are essential to providing an environment in which stable relationships can exist and grow. *These same stable relationships will most likely produce people who are able to trust others and be trusted themselves.*

Healthy Marriages

The same principle of falling into the trap of following the norms in one's life, as with family, can be said of marriages. We either learned or failed to learn something about the marriage relationship from our parents' marriage relationship.

If our parents had a good or bad marriage that taught us lessons accordingly. If we were reared in a single-parent-home or were reared by a grandparent instead of a parent, that influenced what we learned. For example: In general, people whose parents never fought in front of them or fought poorly in front of them, either did not learn *how* to "fight" with their spouses in a good way or in any way at all. This might result in mimicking bad behavior or avoiding arguments in most cases and simply being passive-aggressive toward their spouses until there is a blowup. The possible troubling scenarios are numerous if one does not have a frame of reference or understanding of some kind of a healthy relationship.

If this is your story, don't despair, you can learn as well as anyone else to develop the relationship you want. There are hundreds of books, thousands of magazine and online articles available, as well as professional counselors, marriage mentors, and more in your area. (In the appendix I have prepared a list of books I feel would be helpful.) But for now, allow me help paint a picture of what a healthy marriage relationship should resemble.

In the journal article, "Characteristics of long-term first marriages," by D. L. Fenell, he provides us with a list of the ten most important marital characteristics in long-term successful marriages. They were identified by the following:

1. Lifetime commitment to marriage
2. Loyalty to spouse
3. Strong moral values
4. Respect for spouse as a friend
5. Commitment to sexual fidelity
6. Desire to be a good parent
7. Faith in God and spiritual commitment

8. Desire to please and support spouse
9. Good companion to spouse
10. Willingness to forgive and be forgiven

Although this is not an all-encompassing list of traits one should hope for in a marriage, it is a good foundation. I would prefer to look at these, as foundational traits, not ordered according to importance or trying to rank them in any fashion. This is not about trying to do the "big" things and hoping that will be sufficient, nor what the author had in mind. *The goal is building a complete, or whole, relationship that is healthy enough that trust in one another can be restored and flourish.* Each of these important ingredients is common to a healthy marriage relationship. Each of these will add to the overall health of the marriage relationship and would be worthwhile pursuits.

Healthy Relationships and Deeper Issues

If you are the injured party in a breach of trust, either with a family member, a teenage or older child, a co-worker, or a friend, especially if it was in your marriage, you are likely to be offended by what I am about to say *unless* you hear me out completely. Here we go. Let me begin by saying what we would term a "normal" relationship would be where each person is in full control over his or her mind and actions and not suffering from a severe personality disorder that would cause their thinking or behavior to deviate from what would be expected from your average person. That being the case, although the other person in the relationship hurt you and broke your trust, you almost certainly bear *some responsibility for the state of the relationship prior to the offense.* Author and therapist Joshua Coleman, Ph.D., writes, "As a couples' therapist, I have observed that the most important predictor of rebuilding trust after an affair, other than love, is the capacity for both members of the couple to take some responsibility for what happened."

This is usually accurate unless you were actively trying to change the direction of the relationship and the other person had actively resisted your efforts. When I say "actively", I mean you had been doing something to alter its course for extended period—not just making occasional efforts. Just thinking about it or knowing it needed work is not the same. Yes, the other person did what he did because he chose to; *no one is blaming you for someone else's actions.* Just the same, owning the fact you were part of an unhealthy relationship, or a part of allowing it to deteriorate, and it was out of that unhealthy relationship that the hurt came, will actually help you in moving forward and in building a better relationship. Those who take no responsibility whatsoever for the state of the relationships, and completely demonize the other person, have little hope of rebuilding those relationships.

Healthy Relationships Are Built by "Safe People"

Let's begin with the type of people best suited for a healthy relationship. Referring again to the book, *Safe People*, by Cloud and Townsend, reflect on what they have to say, "Safe people are individuals who draw us closer to being the people God intended us to be. Though not perfect, they are 'good enough' in their own character that the net effect of their presence in our lives is positive. They are accepting, honest, and present, and they help us bear good fruit in our lives."

Additionally, they can be confronted with their behavior without an adverse reaction, they are "repentant" when in the wrong because they do not want to be the kind of person who does wrong. They are "motivated by love to not hurt anyone like that again." If this does not describe either you or the other person in your relationship or both, this would be a good place to start on building a good foundation for a healthy relationship.

Healthy Relationships Are Stable and Supportive

If I am in a relationship where trust has the potential to be restored, I am *not* concerned that I might be:

1. Abandoned, either emotionally or physically
2. Never forgiven for my failures, but will have to hear about them for years to come
3. Constantly criticized for my personality, wants, likes, dislikes, or opinions, etc.
4. Forbidden to disagree with the other without being told that I am, or my point of view is stupid
5. Wanting to grow as a person *in the way I feel best*

It would be easy to continue with the list, but I want to point out the characteristics of a healthy trusting relationship. That is the easy part. In that example, stress and anxiety related to the relationship would be gone. It would be just the opposite of the above list. For example:

1. I would know I would not be abandoned, either emotionally or physically
2. I would know I would be forgiven for my failures and they would not be used against me
3. I would know I would not be constantly criticized for my personality, wants, likes, dislikes, or opinions, etc.

4. I would know I could disagree with the other person without being told that I am, or my point of view is stupid
5. I would know I could seek to grow as a person *in the way I felt best*

Now apply that mindset to your relationship that has suffered a break in the trust or in the one you want to keep strong. Wouldn't you say forgiving or being forgiven would be easier in a stable and supportive relationship? To be in a relationship where one can be vulnerable or can let down one's defenses without worry is an ideal situation. Jane Collingwood explained it like this,

> Securely attached people tend to have positive views of their relationships, often reporting a great deal of satisfaction in their relationships. They feel comfortable both with intimacy and with independence, seeking to balance the two. When they do feel anxious, they try to reduce their anxiety by seeking physical or psychological closeness to their partner. During difficult situations they seek support, comfort, and assistance from their partner. A secure partner then responds positively, reaffirming a sense of normality and reducing anxiety.

There is nothing so good in a relationship as knowing the other person shares a bond with you that is greater than anyone's failures or inadequacies. It frees us up to be a better "us" and a better "us" can add immeasurably to the relationship and to the well-being of the other person.

When working on a relationship where the trust was broken, I sometimes see people confuse their journey with their destination. In other words, they have struggled for so long in a situation they begin to think this is all there is for them. It does take longer than we like to rebuild trust or create a new normal or a healthy relationship; however, just remember the problems you are experiencing are not all that is meant for your life. Good things await you!

Chapter Fourteen

Learning to Connect
in a Healthy Way

· · · · · ·

There is sometimes a tendency in some relationships for those involved to rush the reconciliation for the sake of getting past the pain and back to a sense of normalcy. However, remember there is a tendency among humans to fall back into the same habits of thought and behavior. This is not to say that another break in trust is likely to happen, but if all that has taken place is the cooling of anger and some soothing of pain, and forgiveness is within reach, the relaxed atmosphere could lead to just getting back to life as normal. Resist this drift because it was during life as "normal" that the breach in trust took place. Restoring trust in a relationship requires more than the "putting out of fires" that have flared up. Trust requires a true connection that is the result of a great deal of work on the relationship in addition to apologies and forgiveness.

The effort involved in achieving this true connection requires a continual commitment to healthy communication, emotional support, and sensitivity to the needs of the other, good boundaries, and many more elements that are essential. The good news is that much of this effort will not feel like an effort once healthy communication and emotional connection is formed. In fact, many often feel happy about working on their relationship and look forward to learning more about the other person and getting closer to them. However, before we get to that point we have a few items on our "to-do" list. Let's start with the most objectionable.

Unquestionable Commitment

People feel a much higher level of comfort trying to connect with people who show a genuine commitment to them. It's disconcerting to extend oneself to another not knowing if the feelings and actions are going to be reciprocated.

What if you are the one who betrayed another? Most people who have betrayed someone they love feel plagued by feelings of guilt, sadness, shame, or remorse. Your own capacity to hurt a loved one may also damage your own self-esteem and identity.

Joshua Coleman, Ph.D., writes, "If you have betrayed someone you love, the following steps are crucial.

> **Take complete responsibility for your actions.** No matter how driven you felt to have the affair, nobody made you do it.
>
> **Assume it will take time for your partner to heal.** Your feelings of guilt, shame, or humiliation may make you reluctant to raise the topic of the affair or, when raised, cause you to close down the conversation prematurely . . . You should be prepared to maintain ongoing, sometimes painful conversations about your betrayal.

Be empathic. Your guilt and shame may make you uncomfortable listening to how badly you've made your partner feel. However, it is critical that you show empathy and make amends for how much hurt you've caused your partner.

Respect the need for new limits or rules. Your partner has good reasons to be more suspicious than he or she was prior to the event. Accept that there should now be more transparency around emails, phone logs, and so on. The less defensive you are, the more quickly your relationship will heal as trust is reestablished.

Show enthusiasm for change and repair. Your partner may doubt that you want to change. If you really want to show that you are worth trusting, you will have to demonstrate that you are in it for the long haul.

Genuine Relationships

Connecting with others always has an element of uncertainty if we suspect the other person is not genuine in some way. In general, people like those whom they consider "real" or authentic in their words, actions, intentions, and expression of feelings. That genuineness adds a comfort level to the relationship because we feel we know what we are getting with that relationship and person. Writing on what he calls the "Three Attributes of Trust," David Lansky, PhD., offers this,

Families and individuals who are able to sustain a culture of mutual trust, generally adhere to three basic elements, whether intentionally or not:

1. Individuals are reliable. They do what they say they will do.
2. They demonstrate feelings of intimacy. They care about each other and generally like being together.
3. They are honest with each other. They have open, direct communication—they are willing to speak and to listen when difficult things need to be said.

Those who want trusting and healthy relationships must remove all ambiguity about who one is, and what another can expect from him. Saying to another, "If you love me you will trust me" is a lame and pathetic plea for faith in a person. You and I both probably know people we love and care about, but do not trust what they will do or say. Genuineness is solid ground on which trust can be built—anything else looks risky.

Mutual Respect

Respect is usually lost or at least damaged in a breach of trust. However, those who rebuild the trust will naturally rebuild the respect. With this rebuilt mutual respect, they may even find that they have a depth in their relationship that they never had before. The key to achieving this is working to maintain the balance in the relationship. No one person can have the upper hand in the relationship. This gives them an advantage and in some cases control in the relationship.

Control is an uneasy topic with some who are at odds due to trust being broken. It's not just rebellious or unwise teens that get themselves in trouble by proving untrustworthy and then lament their parents are being "unreasonable" by controlling where and when they go out. Anytime a person who has messed up in some way gets held accountable, thereafter you might hear them protest,

"You're trying to control me!" This can even happen when a person who always gets her way is challenged or questioned. Nevertheless, accountability is not controlling and mutual respect calls for accountability.

Additionally, mutual respect cannot be achieved if one person is offering uninhibited forgiveness when the other person barely acknowledges his or her wrong or if one repents in tears and humility and the other is reluctant or disdainful or even reserved in the forgiveness offered. This is not the sign of mutual respect and everyone deserves a measure of respect as a person.

Creating a Bond

Life teaches us that the more experiences we share with others the closer we feel to the ones with whom we have shared those experiences. When we laugh together, experience new things together, hurt together, and even weep together, the power of the shared experience often becomes the power of the shared bond. One of the best explanations of how a couple can build this bond comes from the work of John Gottman in his book, *Seven Principles for Making Marriage Work*. With a little adjustment, the principles would help any relationship. Gottman likens it to building a "Sound Relationship House." The steps to building this relationship house are as follows:

1. **Build Love Maps:** How well do you know your partner's inner psychological world, his or her history, worries, stresses, joys, and hopes?
2. **Share Fondness and Admiration:** The antidote for contempt, this level focuses on the amount of affection and

respect within a relationship. (To strengthen fondness and admiration, express appreciation and respect.)

3. **Turn Towards:** State your needs, be aware of bids for connection and turn towards them. The small moments of everyday life are actually the building blocks of relationship.

4. **The Positive Perspective:** The presence of a positive approach to problem-solving and the success of repair attempts.

5. **Manage Conflict:** We say "manage" conflict rather than "resolve" conflict, because relationship conflict is natural and has functional, positive aspects. Understand that there is a critical difference in handling perpetual problems and solvable problems.

6. **Make Life Dreams Come True:** Create an atmosphere that encourages each person to talk honestly about his or her hopes, values, convictions and aspirations.

7. **Create Shared Meaning:** Understand important visions, narratives, myths, and metaphors about your relationship.

These steps will help you to put your relationship first in your life and be able to reap the benefits. I recommend getting the book.

Maintaining Good Boundaries

Boundaries in our society seem to be going the way of the dinosaur. This is playing havoc with people's relationships. Connecting in a healthy way also requires good boundaries so we do not connect with others in an *unhealthy* way. Below are some examples of healthy boundaries that help prevent unhealthy connections I have gleaned from wise people over the years:

- Don't be flirtatious with other people. Even playfulness with the right person will send the wrong message.
- Always wear your engagement or wedding ring.
- Set limits on social networking sites or share an account. Always remain accountable for everything said or done on these sites.
- Close relationships with a member of the opposite sex outside one's marriage are a bad idea. Even if "nothing is going on" you will be tempted to confide in or share with someone other than your spouse. If your spouse "doesn't like to," or doesn't "want to" talk, see a counselor and work on your relationship.
- Likewise, there are no good reasons for still having a previous boyfriend's or girlfriend's number programmed in your cell phone or for texting him/her on a regular basis. *Sometimes* there's no choice with a former spouse, but there is with a person one has dated.
- Don't keep any relationships a secret from one's spouse.
- Don't involve one's family (i.e., parents, siblings, Aunt Myrtle) in one's marriage.
- Don't unburden your heart to others about things you dislike in your partner. People outside your relationship should stay outside your relationship.
- Talk things over before spending or give away "our" money.
- Don't yell. Nothing good happens once the yelling begins.
- Violence is unacceptable. No debate. End of subject.

There are so many more good boundaries one can have; even so, it's not possible to carry around an all-encompassing list. In light of this, stick to the Golden Rule: *Treat others the way you want to be treated.* (See Matthew 7:12.)

A Commitment to Overcome

Teaming up with another to overcome an obstacle is a great way to build a connection with that person. There is something about a shared experience, whether good or bad. Teammates build relationships that often last for a lifetime. They have shared competition. Olympians, professional athletes, those who have achieved great things academically, or those who simply work the same job—each share a story with those who had a similar experience. Even in experiences of hardship we see it. Cancer survivors have a connection because of what they have shared. You see it in survivors of disease and disaster and war. Sharing a struggle helps people connect. Even prisoners build bonds—they have shared a similar adversity. Yes, even those who share the story of broken trust, and getting past it, can build a strong bond. That is, *IF* they choose to overcome the obstacles they face.

Louella Vaz gives us a list of barriers or obstacles people face in rebuilding or having trust in their relationships. *Learning to connect in a healthy way requires we overcome these obstacles:*

1. Desire to control—the situation where one person in a relationship attempts to control the actions, thoughts or emotions of another. This clearly results in a situation of unequal position or power.
2. Dishonesty—where one or more individuals are hiding information, providing only half-truths, or are attempting to be purposefully misleading.
3. Self-centeredness—where the focus is on self and one's own needs, wants and desires.
4. Lack of openness—a situation in which one or more persons are not open and free in expressing their opinions, describing their position on issues, or relating information.

5. Communication—is required for trust to develop. Failure to communicate effectively leads to a failure of trust.

6. Empathy—when difficulties in a relationship develop, as will undoubtedly happen, the failure to identify with the troubles experienced by the injured person and willingness to work together to address the problem leads to reduced trust.

7. Positive feelings—focusing on the negatives, becoming jealous of success, or allowing suspicious feelings to fester can all lead to a reduction of trust in others.

Ultimately, being able to trust someone new or who has proven herself fallible requires we believe in that person to some degree—at least in that they want to do us no harm and have good intentions toward us. We also need to know she has the ability and willingness to follow through on her promises or commitments. Getting to know that person would quite naturally be essential as would investing in her, and having good intentions toward her, having our own ability and willingness to follow through on our commitments and promises. It is a union based in cause and effect. An action or event produces a response to the action or event. Connecting in a healthy way requires actions and experiences of a positive nature. A commitment to doing these things will consequently produce a healthy connection.

CHAPTER FIFTEEN

Learning to Trust Again

......

D ouglas McGregor wrote a number of years ago something that is a timeless truth: "Trust is a delicate property of human relationships. It is influenced far more by actions than by words. It takes a long time to build, but it can be destroyed very quickly. Even a single action—perhaps misunderstood—can have powerful effects." Wow. Do you feel the pressure to get it right? Building trust or rebuilding trust can be especially overwhelming for those whose lives may have been filled with poor examples of trustworthy people. Consequently, just the idea of trusting someone is a challenge, and learning to trust someone again after a betrayal may be something outside of reasonable thinking.

Many people find it difficult to trust others in general, so when someone close to them violates their trust it can be devastating. We usually see this with people who have experienced many disappointments and deceptions over a lifetime. Unfortunately, many people's childhood is where they learned to doubt people and expect the worst from them. As I often tell clients, "Whatever environment you grew up in will feel normal, no matter how much you may hate it or do not want it, it will still feel somewhat normal, and we tend to gravitate toward what is normal." If it has always or mostly been one's experience that people aren't trustworthy, learning to trust will be a challenge, and learning to trust someone again will be a bigger challenge.

In a similar fashion, we often feel comfortable with the type of people we grew up around—even if we don't want to be around people like that any longer. When we grew up around people who lied, manipulated, and broke the trust of others, this can often leave us more susceptible to this type of behavior. It doesn't make sense at the time. The thought of our actually allowing someone like that into our lives is offensive. Yet many must accept the possibility that we sometimes inadvertently allow emotionally unhealthy people into our lives. It's not intentional. That's why it is surprising.

Now, that said, allow me to pause and clarify that I am *not* saying a person who is betrayed is the one responsible for any hurts that come her way because she allowed that person in her life. That would be ridiculous. If you and I chose all the wrong people to be in our lives, it would still not give them the right to betray or hurt us.

Nonetheless, we are talking about learning to trust again and that will require examining the path we have taken and the path we will take in our future relationships. For example, I spoke with an elderly woman once (not a client) who recounted to me the same bad experience she had been through with each of her four husbands, concluding that she did not understand why "men were like that" and why she never could find a "good husband." I asked her to describe her father. Oddly, the description she gave sounded like each of her four husbands. I observed that it sounded as if she had married a man like her father each time. Over seventy years flashed through her mind, as she stood there apparently stunned by my observation. Then quietly she replied, "That's what I did . . ."

Even so, that still gave each of those men no right to treat her as they did and in no way did she deserve to be mistreated. Just the same, by her choices she set herself up to be in relationships that would continually destroy her ability or desire to trust another man.

Recognizing People Who Are Easier to Trust

There's a wonderful little book called, *Safe People*, by Dr. Henry Cloud and Dr. John Townsend that everyone should read. There is so much good information in it that there is just too much to try to cover; nevertheless allow me to share some of the helpful bone-jarring truths found in just one chapter on why we end up in relationships where we get hurt.

> How is it that some people seem to have a talent for picking destructive people? Whether in friendship or romance, they seem to always end up getting close to people who hurt them. Are they just unlucky? Are their bad relationships all a result of pure chance?
>
> We do not think so. Although there are instances where innocent people are truly betrayed, when a person has a pattern of being hurt by relationships, it is usually not by chance. When people find themselves in destructive relationship after destructive relationship, they must finally decide that the common denominator connecting all those "bad" people is themselves.

As unpleasant as it may be, many have had to come to grips with the fact that their own character flaws might have been setting them up for hurt in relationships. But let hasten to say again and to clarify, this gives the offender no right to hurt another. However, that being said, we bear a responsibility to be wise in our relationships at all times, especially when we are trying to learn to trust again so that we can once again have satisfying relationships with others.

Now, let's continue with what Cloud and Townsend say are the "character flaws" that set us up to be in relationship with people who are likely to hurt us. The following short summary list will suffice for making the point:

- **Inability to judge character**
- **Isolation and fear of abandonment** (a lack of connection with others)
- **Defensive hope** (thinking the other person will change if we just love them enough or correctly)
- **Unfaced badness** (when our own "badness" is given life through a relationship with another
- **Merger wishes** (trying to make up for our shortcomings by "fusing" our identity with another
- **Fear of confrontation** (the inability or unwillingness to confront the behavior of the other person)
- **Romanticizing** (seeing the other person in an idealized way)
- **Need to rescue** (the other person is so needy they really have nothing to offer; disappointment is headed our way if we are rescuers)
- **Familiarity** (we choose what is unhealthy because it is familiar)
- **Victim role** (when a person ceases to take responsibility for their own choices and behaviors)
- **Guilt** (the other person "makes us feel guilty" when they don't get their way)
- **Perfectionism** (demanding perfection from others)
- **Repetition** (falling into the same pattern over and over again in regard to relationships)
- **Denial of pain and perceptions** (ignoring our feelings, observations, or instincts when we should listen to them)

As you can see, the question of why it is difficult for some to trust others in general is a question with no simple answer. Consequently, maybe declaring "all people" as untrustworthy is a bit premature. Likewise, maybe the world is not against us. Maybe people in general are not out to hurt us? Maybe we have set ourselves up in situations and relationships that just increased the likelihood of us being hurt? Yes, they should not have done what they did. They were wrong. Though, *in some cases*, we must admit we had *a part* in the collapse of trust.

Learning to trust again is about more than finding the right person or a "good person" with whom to be in relationship. It is about learning to develop good, healthy relationships. Maybe finding a new spouse, a new friend, a new coworker, a new family member is not the answer. Maybe developing a healthy relationship with the people who are already in your life and who want to do what is right is the answer.

On the other hand, we can isolate ourselves, become more self-reliant, take on the mindset of believing "no one can be trusted," but at the end of the day we have only hurt ourselves and deprived ourselves of many positive, healthy relationships. Yes, the hurt is hard to forget. At times, we may even find ourselves mulling it over and ruminating on the hurt like a dog chews a bone, savoring it, gnawing at it. Yes, it can seem satisfying—until you realize you are chewing on your own bones.

Learning to Trust Again Takes Time

Learning to trust another person or other persons again is a process that requires a varying amount of time along with some discomfort to be endured on the way to success. Being progressive in nature and not time dependent, in that there is no established timetable for when certain tasks must have been completed, a healthy attitude and a commitment to the process is essential. In a similar way, although ideally requiring participation by all involved, it is nonetheless not entirely person or situation dependent, in that one can make positive advances on a personal level regardless of the level of the other person's participation or the suitability of the situation. At times one may be making more progress or appear to be putting forth more effort than the other. This may alternate over time. Hopefully, all involved will be equally committed, but one can only control himself and his actions. In this instance, he must do what he can. If he cannot restore the relationship because of lack of participation on the part of the other person, he can at least prepare himself to be better able to have other healthy relationships now and in the future.

This will call for one to be flexible and willing to adjust to changing circumstances, feelings, and levels of commitment from the other person. The last thing he should do is to box himself in and mentally create an idealized outcome or take an either/or approach. Sometimes people do this by telling themselves, "If I'm going to trust again I just have to start trusting people *without question*"—not a good idea—or decide the opposite of trusting no one. Trying to trust too much too quickly often generates a constant state of anxiety, and trusting no one usually leads to a cynical, pessimistic, and depressive outlook. Once again, balance in the key.

"Learning" to trust in a healthy manner is the idea here. This is with the assumption that either there was a problem with the previous level of trust or that the breach in trust has left someone uncertain of how to start trusting again. Although this is somewhat of a review of some of the material we have covered, please indulge me. There are several areas of great importance when seeking to develop a new approach to trusting or in starting over.

For all who are involved there is the common need for each to work to raise his/her level of self-awareness. It's too tempting to try to apologize or forgive and quickly move on in order to minimize the pain. Please slow down a bit if that is your approach. There is a need to try to understand what has happened in *your* relationship. How did you contribute, if in any way? Ponder your own motives, feelings, needs, possible failings, behavior, and communication style or lack of communication. Everyone needs to examine himself for mistakes or misunderstandings. Everyone should ask himself some hard questions.

The assignment of blame is not the goal here. We are learning to trust again. In doing so, we must know ourselves and be honest with ourselves so that we can be honest with others. The unspoken and the unknown, as well as the avoided topics and evasive maneuvers designed to avoid open, honest discussions have to go. If not, the previous cycle of behavior will threaten to return and undermine the process of developing trust. We cannot connect emotionally with anyone with whom we cannot be honest about ourselves or one we fear will reject us.

Learning to Trust Again Requires Wisdom

Learning to trust again may mean learning to trust in new ways, with new boundaries, and new expectations. It often means learning to understand and accept the weaknesses of people including ourselves. For instance, some people aren't responsible with money—is that a reason to allow the relationship to be destroyed? Couldn't adjustments be made? Some people are out for number one, and their self-awareness is so low they don't see it. As long as those in relationship with the person realize this to be someone who will *always put their own* interests before anyone else's, a friendship can still exist. Some teens, maybe more than some, are irresponsible and by adult standards make impulsive, unwise decisions. Is that any reason to label one's child a failure, a problem child, worthless or to stop trying to be involved in her life? Some spouses have what appears to be a flirtatious personality, making many spouses angry. All the same, is that any reason to divorce them if they are willing to try to change?

My point is if we eliminate everyone who fails us in any measure we will soon find ourselves alone, and isolated, and likely cynical. Unless you want to be a crotchety old hermit or known as the crazy old cat lady on the street that has forty-five cats and no human friends, learning to trust in new ways would be worth a try. All I'm saying is try it with a good dose of wisdom.

Expect "Flashbacks"

Essentially a "flashback" is an experience that takes place in a moment when one suddenly remembers a traumatic event almost as if he or she is experiencing it again. There is usually a triggering event setting this experience in motion. People who have been deeply hurt on an emotional level through the deceit or betrayal of a trusted individual may experience moments similar to a flashback. Some instances in a person that might initiate this experience is having been abandoned by another, having been physically harmed by someone who one thought would keep her safe, or having had a spouse be unfaithful. There are too many possible experiences to cover, but consider a brief—and simple—explanation of each of these.

Abandoned: Just the word sounds lonely and hurtful. Imagine a child who trusts his parent in spite of what adults know is a history of irresponsible behavior. In spite of all of the parent's faults the child loves and idealizes the parent. Over the years serving as a pastor and counselor, I have been amazed at how a mistreated child will still crave a relationship with an abusive parent. A child doesn't understand adult issues. A child only wants the love of Mom and Dad and to feel safe and loved. A child will hope against all hope and love without good reason. Now let that parent or parents continually disappear from that child's life and return, disappear and return. Even if the parent(s) "get their act together", if there is the slightest hint of the behavior pattern that previously preceded their past disappearances, that child will usually experience anxiety about the possibility the parents will abandon her again. Even with the parent(s) being responsible, the child will have to learn to trust them again.

Consider the person harmed. A simple example could be a child or adult who has trusted another significant person in his or her life. That person goes through a period of not controlling his or her anger and slaps the trusting individual on multiple occasions. Even if the angry person reforms, until trust is reestablished, every time that person becomes angry, the victim will become concerned, cautious, and possibly withdrawn. Becoming angry and yelling at the previously victimized person, "I'm not going to hit you! Why can't you let that go?" actually doesn't help.

Now to the offense that seems to keep on giving long after everyone would rather have forgotten it—infidelity. Take the case of John and Jane Doe: Jane had an affair with another man almost six months ago. John has worked to forgive and move on and Jane is grateful for his patience, at least most of the time. Part of the issue is that John, being an analytical person by nature, needed "all the facts" about the affair. When I say all the facts, I mean he wanted every minuscule detail. Jane was just grateful he was willing to forgive and gave him everything for which he asked. Both have come to regret it.

Now, when they drive by the restaurant where Jane would meet the other man, John's memory is triggered and the emotions start flowing. When she is late and doesn't call—something she did a great deal of during the affair—John's memory is triggered and he feels the need to track her down. In fact, anytime Jane does or says anything that reminds John of the past events it seems he has a flashback. For months now it's like John has bought a house on Memory Lane. Part of the problem is his tendency to obsess, part is he asked too many questions about details that didn't matter, and part of the issue is that at times Jane gets a little tired of feeling she is under constant surveillance.

The good news is they love one another. Both struggle with trying to get it right. John is a little embarrassed he overreacts and is so paranoid. Jane is sad she had such a major role in the creation of the situation. Jane must accept that it will take time for her to prove she can be trusted again, not because she is doing anything wrong, but because what was broken hasn't been repaired. She must not seek to justify past wrongs or irresponsible behavior when she feels John is "taking it too far." This only inspires John to force her on a tour of Memory Lane. John needs to see a neutral party like a professional counselor to help him get a grip because he can't forget short of having a severe blow to the head—which she has considered in moments of frustration—yet knows in her heart he is trying.

John needs to take the advice I heard somewhere, "You didn't choose to bring the other man into your relationship, but you can choose to keep him out!" John must take his own steps to keep the other man out of his marriage, in thought, in words, and in any other way, *he* figuratively brings the other man into the relationship. Next, John must keep in mind that *if there is no real justification* for saying there has been another violation of trust, there is no need to go down Memory Lane.

Learning to trust again is possible and is made easier by understanding what is going on with one's feelings and emotions. For example, we must first learn to recognize illogical thoughts and behaviors as well as an emotionally driven state of mind before we are able to challenge them. Working together toward the same goal and maintaining a forgiving and gracious attitude will greatly help.

Rebuilding Trust Is a Joint Effort

It is not an uncommon occurrence for someone to complain the person whom they let down won't trust him even though he has apologized and not done that particular misdeed again. Teens and spouses are especially prone to this it seems—maybe it's the family connection. Either way, the problem usually stems from the fact they haven't given up all misleading or unreliable behavior. Just as we want to try to trust someone we love, we also want that person to attempt to remove all doubt of his intentions. Otherwise, the fear is he is going to disappoint us in a new way.

To remove this uncertainty there has to be some give-and-take on behalf of both parties. For instance, this might work in the following way if I were to break your trust:

- You would choose to take a realistic perspective concerning who I am and what I am able to do or to become as a person, and I will do everything I can to justify that respect shown to me.
- You would accept me in a loving, caring manner as I am, and in return I will commit to trying to grow as a person.
- You will assume I am telling you the truth and I will try to do nothing that will cause you to doubt me.

- I will acknowledge, without excuse, that you have the right to be hurt or angry and will not use my response as justification for not trying to make amends.
- We will talk openly and honestly with one another with no one threatening or implying the other will be rejected for being honest.
- We will accept one another "warts and all."
- We will be patient and kind to one another and commit to removing all fear from the relationship.
- We will work to grow on a personal level and support the other in doing the same.

A commitment to one another is the glue that will hold the relationship together in tough times. Of course, there must also be love, forgiveness, respect, honesty, mutual trust, and more; however, being *committed to work together* on rebuilding the trust is essential. I cannot control you and you cannot control me. We would each need to control ourselves and each need to put a little faith in the other. The goal at this point is not 100 percent of trust. That can happen with time. For now, we are learning to trust again. Next, we will work on learning to connect.

Working Together to Rebuild Trust

Rebuilding trust in a relationship is clearly a joint effort involving everyone who is a part of the relationship in question. This may include a family, a couple, or a friendship, just to name a few of the possible relationship pairings. As with all joint efforts, clear and effective communication is essential. Whoever is involved must be actively working toward the same goal in the same way at the same time if there is any hope of resolving the issues present in that relationship.

Far too often I see a couple, or family, or friends who report working to resolve the same issue and yet meeting with failure. In most cases, what is happening is that each person is going about resolving the perceived issue in a different way and usually not at the same time. This becomes apparent as the misunderstandings increase and the inconsistencies in progress continue, resulting in an inability to resolve the issue(s).

Some would say those involved are not on the same page. To extend the "same page" analogy, my contention is that those involved need to not only get on the same page, but also make sure they are focused on the same paragraph on the same page and even make sure they are reading the same sentence in the same paragraph.

As a means of getting everyone to that starting point, I would like to suggest a simple three-step plan. In order for this to happen there will need to be a conversation with the person or persons involved in which a great deal of clarification takes place. Each of the following steps will help in finding that clarity:

- **Step one: What is our goal?** Do not assume just because someone is in relationship with you or that you are working on the same issue that the goal will be the same. For instance, if someone has broken your trust, he or she may want to be the kind of person you will be able to trust again, but he or she may just want to get you "off their back." One might say, "My goal is to not be questioned constantly about everything I do." Another might say, "I want to know that you are different." Do not make the mistake of thinking this person is working for the same goal. One wants freedom from scrutiny. The other wants a person who will not disappoint him again in the same way.

If each pursues his or her own goal, the two will *not* end up at the same destination.

Suggestions:
1. Ask for a clear goal from the other person and then state your goal.
2. Each should ask specific questions of the other for clarification.
3. Write down the agreed-upon goal.

- **Step two: How are we going to reach our goal?** This is an instance where people may assume the other person is considering the same solution. This is not usually the case.

If we stick with the different goals used as examples in the explanation of "step one" we can easily see the problem here. The first person says, "My goal is to not be questioned constantly about everything I do." That person's solution for reaching her goal may be for the other person to just stop mentioning the issue, or "drop it." The only assurance she may offer to the other person might be, "I told you that you could trust me. I said I wouldn't do it again. Just leave me alone and I will show you." In this instance, the first person is rejecting any idea of personal accountability and is not showing any real interest in helping the other person to feel better about the relationship. This is a recipe for failure.

The questions for the first person are as follows:

- Is it reasonable to expect no questions from a person with whom you have a relationship?
- How are you going to "show" you are trustworthy?
- What are you going to do to help reduce the anxiety of the other person?

Now, consider our second person's goal, "I want to know that you are different." That sounds reasonable; however, we must ask him, "What do you mean 'different'" and "What is it that you want to see?"

In this instance, the second person has left the goal so vague a misunderstanding is certainly to take place. It usually happens something like this: The first person behaves herself, as she sees it, but then she is questioned about something she has done or said, provoking feelings of resentment in her. *(Remember her goal was to not be questioned.)* The conversation that follows erupts in anger and the first person screams, "I'm tired of this! You're never going to trust me no matter how hard I try!"

This accusation is followed by the second person firing back, "How can I trust you when you won't answer my questions, you won't call when you're going to be late, you aren't where you say you're going to be, and you don't talk to me except when you want something. It's like you're hiding something!" (Remember, his goal was to know the other person was "different.")

Did the second person ever tell the first person what it would take to see her as different or what he meant by "different"? No, that is part of the problem. Evidently, if the other person were to show herself to be different she would need to at least do the following:

- Answer all his questions
- Call when she is going to be late
- Be where she says she's going to be
- Communicate more with him
- Don't act as if she is hiding something

Suggestions:
1. Agree on solutions or a plan of action that both accept.
2. Agree upon specific actions each will take.

3. Agree upon changes in behavior or communication each will make.

- **Step three: When do we begin?** Sounds simple enough, but never underestimate someone's ability to misunderstand or, in some cases, wriggle out of his/her responsibilities.

Allow me to give an example of something similar to what I have heard numerous times.

"We agreed we would go to counseling, but he never made an appointment," one might say.

"You never said who you wanted to go see, or where, or when you wanted me to make the appointment," the other defends.

The result in the preceding example might be that they never go to counseling, or it's months later when they do, and so much hostility has built up that it will take twice as long to get them back on track. Again, being specific would have helped. A time frame for beginning might look something like this:

- **Seeking counseling?** Sit down and look at your options immediately. Both check your schedule, find a counselor, and set an appointment.
- **Trying to establish financial responsibility? Let us** get our credit cards out and decide which ones we can cut up and no longer use. **Let us** do a budget. **Let us** decide how much we will spend this month on clothes, entertainment, etc., or better yet, **let us** seek qualified financial counseling.
- **Setting and agreeing to a curfew?** This is the new time to be home *every* night starting today. Any changes must be agreed to at least one day prior to the change—*unless we can verify* there is an emergency or a problem—and we will verify it. Understood?

- **Putting a stop to inappropriate relationships?** I expect you to delete her number from your phone, email address, or any other contact information right now—not when you "have time."

These are but examples that each would need to adjust for his or her specific situation, but the idea in the early stage of rebuilding trust is to clarify messages and meanings and intentions on a consistent basis. This will work if those involved will give the other permission to ask relevant questions. I say "relevant" because it can easily turn into an interrogation with some people. This is why it is important to know the goal, the plan, and the time for action. Questions asked about those established measures will most likely be relevant and less likely to be considered critical.

Chapter Sixteen

Keep Your Goal in Sight

· · · · · ·

A t this point you may be sold on the idea that forgiveness and the restoration of trust are what you want for your relationship. Does it feel like something deep down inside is still eating at you? It might be the last remnants of the human desire for a reckoning. It's that feeling that the account books still feel a little out of balance. There hasn't been a full accounting for what has been done. It's a feeling that will sneak up on you just when you think it is all settled and the wrestling with feelings of hurt begins again. Perhaps you're on the other side of the fence and wonder if the other person will ever forgive you no matter how much you apologize or try to atone for your mistake. Maybe you are wondering if the person you hurt will ever allow you out from under the weight of the guilt you feel. Will he ever stop using it against you? *Don't give up. You're almost there. Whether the relationship is salvaged or not, your freedom from this hurt must be gained!*

Without freedom from this hurtful experience, it will be too easy to allow the events of the past to define you and determine what you will do in the future. Learning to trust again is the goal, not reconciling everything that has happened, not going into a protective shell where we hope to never be hurt or disappointed again. The goal is not trying to analyze the other person. It's not about coming up with a plan or a set of rules to protect oneself. It's not about being perfect. The ultimate goal is trust. The essential goal is freedom.

Jean Otto writes, "Have some of your carefully created castles been washed away? Mine have. Several times along my life's journey, I had nowhere to turn except into my heavenly Father's arms. There I remained quiet, soaking up his love for as long as I needed. Then I saw his hand begin a new creation for my life, a new direction, a new service for him and his kingdom. Waves need not always destroy. We must allow our heavenly Father to use them to redirect our lives."

This Is No Time for Fatalism

What one must remember is there is hope. It is possible for a person to prove himself to the person he betrayed, but he must intentionally work together with the other person. Yes, *sometimes* it doesn't work out the way we hoped, but giving in to fatalism is the decision to give up hope and cease to try based on feelings and not the facts. In this sense, fatalism would be the belief that someone is powerless to change himself or a situation. There are ways one can empower himself. No, it's not always easy, but neither is living a fatalistic existence in which one feels his or her life is beyond control or hope.

If you have experienced a break in the trust of your relationship, let me encourage you not to dwell on the failure and not to allow it to become your identity. There is no value in forever seeing oneself as an adulterer, loser, victim, cheat, or as one who is "messed up" or "broken" or as someone who "couldn't make her marriage work." The one who broke the trust needs to apologize and do all that is possible to make amends. The person wronged should work to forgive, for her own sake if for no other reason, and move forward taking the necessary steps to find healing. You are not your failure.

I love the affirmation Christian author and minister Max Lucado wrote in his book, *On the Anvil.* He writes, "Today I will make a difference. I will not let past failures haunt me. Even though my life is scarred with mistakes, I refuse to rummage through my trash heap of failures. I will admit them. I will correct them. I will press on. Victoriously. No failure is fatal. It's OK to stumble. I will get up. It's OK to fail. I will rise again. Today I will make a difference." Reject that fatalistic mindset. You don't have time for it. You have a life to live and a difference to make.

The goal started out to be, and hopefully still is, to heal the hurt and restore the broken trust. Keep working toward that. Feelings, arguments, disappointments, setbacks, and even the thoughts and opinions of others will threaten to take you off course and cause you to miss your goal of restoring trust. As a result, you should examine everything you feel like doing or saying in light of that goal. When feelings are strong and uncertainty prevails, there is wisdom in slowing down. It may feel as if you have no control, and maybe you cannot control others or circumstances, but you can control yourself. Slowing down and getting control of yourself and your thoughts will do more to empower you and keep you from saying or doing something unwise than anything else. Spend some time alone in meditation or prayer or just go for a walk and think. Find what helps *you* relax. Realign your thoughts and set your mind on the goal once again and then ask yourself, *"Will what I want to say or do help me reach my goal of restoring trust?"* Having done this you will be better prepared to continue the work of forgiveness, and forgiveness is a work that will pay off big in the end.

The Willingness to *Trust* the One Who Hurt Is Not a Sign of Weakness

It's a natural instinct for us as humans to protect ourselves. Consequently, we often become fixated on not being hurt again or taken advantage of again once we have felt the sting of betrayal. No one wants to be or feel weak. The ironic thing is that it is possible for a person to invest so much thought and energy protecting himself relationally that he hurts himself relationally. A well-known Presbyterian minister, speaker, and columnist from the early 1900s, Dr. Frank Crane, presents us with an apparent dilemma when he wrote, "You may be deceived if you trust too much, but you will live in torment if you don't trust enough."

Balance remains a key consideration in almost all areas. Of course regaining one's balance after someone has broken your trust and left you feeling deceived, used, or taken advantage of is often easier said than done. It requires great strength and courage to extend oneself again to the person who hurt you or to others who could potentially hurt you. The unknown makes it so scary and difficult. This is even more reason to see those who move forward with forgiveness as strong and not weak. The fallback position where one can gather strength and regain resolve can be found in part in Reinhold Niebuhr's popular *Serenity Prayer*.

The Serenity Prayer

God grant me the serenity to accept the things I cannot change; courage to change the things I can; and wisdom to know the difference. Living one day at a time; enjoying one moment at a time; accepting hardships as the pathway to peace; taking, as He did, this sinful world as it is, not as I would have it; trusting that He will make all things right if I surrender to His Will; that I may be reasonably happy in this life and supremely happy with Him forever in the next. Amen.

Forgiving Is Not a Sign of Weakness

Often people express that they feel if they forgive a certain wrong, or forgive too easily, they will be playing the role of a sucker, or the other person will see them as weak and likely mistreat them again. This type of thinking is the kind of thought process that gives the other person power over you. It is also a self-protective mindset. Ironically, it will hurt you more than help you. Understanding the power and benefits of forgiving is essential for one's emotional well-being and ability to move forward.

Looking to Dr. Lewis Smedes again, consider his wisdom in this matter. He writes:

1. Forgiving is the only way to be fair to yourself after someone hurts you unfairly.
2. Forgivers are not doormats; they do not have to tolerate the bad things that they forgive.
3. Forgivers are not fools; they forgive and heal themselves, but they do not have to go back for more abuse.
4. We don't have to wait until the other person repents before we forgive him or her and heal ourselves.
5. Forgiving is a journey. For us, it takes time, so be patient and don't get discouraged if you backslide and have to do it over again.

And remember this: The first person who gets the benefit of forgiving is always the person who does the forgiving. When you forgive a person who wronged you, you set a prisoner free, and then you discover that the prisoner you set free is you. When you forgive, you walk hand in hand with the very God who forgives you everything for the sake of his Son. When you forgive, you heal the hurts you never should have felt in the first place.

The willingness to forgive is actually a personal strength! Choosing to forgive empowers us. The goal is to be free of the hurt and burden of holding a wrong against another.

Forgiving Is Not Condoning or Excusing

Some people have a way of taking our forgiveness and trying to turn it into a get-out-of-jail-free card. Once we utter those magic words—"I forgive you"—they act as if the past is erased! Forgiveness doesn't erase the past; instead it is only saying, "I won't hold it against you any longer." This is *not* the same as overlooking it. We're *not* saying it wasn't a big deal or it was meaningless. The people who do this to the one offering forgiveness are often looking for relief from the guilt. They want to feel free of any responsibility for any hurt that took place. This is one reason some are hesitant to forgive. They are concerned the person will just discount the whole event or reduce it in his mind to a misunderstanding. Think about a couple of scenarios and ask yourself if you have seen this at work.

First, there are those people who apologize, not necessarily to take responsibility for the wrong, but apparently to keep the peace. This person just wants to shut the other person up. He is avoidant and rarely wants to deal with the deeper issues or to take a good long look in the mirror. *Second, there are those who apologize when obviously caught and there is no way out.* These people come in *two varieties*: those who are just giving up the fight and those who sucker punch the person to whom he is apologizing after the apology. The latter is done by adding, "But what you did was just as bad or worse," pulling something up from the past, or he may add, "But I only did it because you . . ." ultimately blaming the other person for his actions. *Thirdly, there are those who said they were sorry but have found their homemade get-out-of-jail-free card doesn't work.* Their approach goes something like this, "How can you say you have forgiven me when you still worry about me doing . . . ?" These people act as if any future expectations or concerns nullify your forgiveness. It is almost as if they are saying, "You're not actually going to hold me accountable, are you?"

Forgiving is not carelessly dismissing our concerns, acting as if we have amnesia, or saying to the other person do whatever, whenever, with whomever, I won't be concerned or ever question you. Keep the goal in sight for both of you if necessary. Reestablishing trust requires collaborating efforts.

Forgiveness Produces Personal Growth

Often, a person who has not forgiven another will be holding on to the wrong, or as we say, holding a grudge. This leads to bitterness and anger. This also often leads to a decline in feeling well physically or emotionally or a decline in overall health. Some even find they have developed a problem with drinking too much. An article by the *Mayo Clinic* cites some of the benefits of forgiving someone that I think you will find will also result in your being able to work things out with the other person as time passes. The same benefits are available to the one needing forgiveness as well. This is one more reason to seek forgiveness. To begin with,

Letting go of grudges and bitterness can make way for compassion, kindness and peace. Forgiveness can lead to:

- Healthier relationships
- Greater spiritual and psychological well-being
- Less anxiety, stress, and hostility
- Lower blood pressure
- Fewer symptoms of depression
- Lower risk of alcohol and substance abuse

The absence of forgiveness, either because one has not sought or received it or has not given it, has a way of causing a person to become mired in unproductive feelings and thought patterns which can stop or slow personal growth. Anyone who has benefited from forgiving another in the ways mentioned will be a person better able to work on his or her relationship. The goal here is to experience personal and relational growth, to be better, more mature, and to get beyond the time of hurt. I hope that trust will be restored. Either way, personal growth and emotional freedom can take place.

You Can Know You Have Forgiven Them

Some years ago I was deeply hurt and disillusioned by the actions of a colleague. In all honesty, I was angry for some time and became bitter over the actions of more than one person. I had trusted this individual and another individual only to find myself betrayed and mistreated. In the grand scheme, all that was hurt was my feelings, but it seemed like much more damage had been inflicted. One day, after I had found it possible to move on and let it go and even forgive, I said to my wife about the events of the past, "You know, it doesn't matter anymore."

Not meaning to minimize my feelings but to put things in perspective, she replied, "You know, it really never did."

I was partially annoyed by her response, thinking she would have said something like, "I'm glad you have gotten past that *terrible* hurt," would have sounded sweeter. After all, a little emotional petting couldn't hurt, right?

"Well," I responded slightly bothered by her response, "Now it doesn't matter to me!"

That's *how I know* I have forgiven someone; it just doesn't matter or hold great meaning to me anymore. It's just a part of my history. I no longer feel angry and hurt. I still remember and still am not happy it happened, but it holds no power over me. I like the way Lewis Smedes explained it. He said, "You will know that forgiveness has begun when you recall those who hurt you and feel the power to wish them well."

Another way one can know forgiveness has taken place is she feels or sees the benefits. In her book, *The Unburdened Heart: 5 keys to forgiveness and freedom*, Mariah Burton Nelson asserts that with practice, forgiveness can become one's daily practice, resulting in the person's experiencing freedom from guilt, shame, pain, anger, and the pain of constantly criticizing other people. Her advice is to offer forgiveness, "regardless of what the other person says or does. Forgive when you're unsure, or afraid, or resentful, or wanting to exact revenge. Forgive when the other person doesn't apologize, or doesn't apologize correctly. Forgive them for that: for their inability, unwillingness, stubbornness, fear."

That is a real challenge for the person who has been hurt by the breach of trust because most feel the offender plays a key role in the process of forgiveness, yet that is where so many become bound and their freedom is lost. Some will never appear sorry, some will never say it, and some as Nelson said, will not "apologize correctly." Amazingly, I have even witnessed some instances where the offender tried desperately to make things right, but the injured party would have none of it. Either way, this is about moving forward. Remember your goal is to forgive or to be forgiven and rebuild the trust if possible. If all that can be done is offering one's forgiveness or repentance, at least freedom from the burden of it all can be found.

Finally, let me give you Nelson's five keys for forgiveness and freedom before we continue:

1. Awareness: Remember who hurt you and how.
2. Validation: Talk to a sympathetic listener.
3. Compassion: Strive to see the offender's humanity.
4. Humility: Reflect on your own faults and failings.
5. Self-forgiveness: Open your heart to yourself.

Remember, it's a Process

Understanding a process can be helpful. It's like a road map to me. Knowing the process helps me stay on track, know where I am, and where I am supposed to be next on my journey. Maybe it will help you to look at the work of rebuilding trust and a relationship in terms of a process. Although all violations of one's trust are hurtful, infidelity is probably the most hurtful of experiences when it comes to a breach of trust. Just the same, restoration of this nature follows a similar process no matter what type of failure has taken place. With this in mind I would suggest the three-stage process from the book, *Helping Couples Get Past the Affair,* by Snyder, Baucom, and Gordon as a good solid approach, whatever your situation.

The first stage of their recovery process is "the impact stage." This is where those involved are working to comprehend what has taken place in the relationship. Absorbing the blow, minimizing any additional damage and regaining a sense of balance are the goals at this point. The second stage is the "meaning stage" in which the event is explored in an attempt to understand why it occurred and frame it in a more understandable context. The third stage is the "moving on stage" where the goal is to find a way to move beyond the event and "no longer allow it to control their lives." This is where the struggle to understand forgiveness is done and where the meaning of forgiveness for the relationship will be decided.

Additionally they add that, "To move forward, the couple needs to achieve three goals by the end of stage 3: (1) Develop a realistic and balanced view of their relationship; (2) experience release from being dominated by negative emotion about the event, with the injured partner voluntarily relinquishing the right to punish the participating partner; and (3) evaluate the relationship carefully and make healthy decisions about its continuation."

I want to pause here and touch on the second of the previous list, "voluntarily relinquishing the right to punish the participating partner," because in my experience if the punishing doesn't stop, the decision about the continuation of the relationship will be made for both. It usually won't continue. By "punishing" I mean the continual act of "throwing it in the face" of the person, constantly bringing it up to justify your attitude or actions, or using it as a "trump card" of sorts to always win an argument or get the other person to back down out of guilt.

For those continuing to punish another out of hurt and anger, accept the fact that this *anger is your problem*. Sure, you might not have had it before the offense, but it is *your* problem now. No matter how much the other person apologizes or changes, *you* must choose to let the anger go. Seek counseling, spiritual guidance, anger management classes, or some means of dealing with it. Secondly, accept that to continue on this course may result in your destroying any hope of the relationship continuing. Finally, realize that for some people who continue to punish the other, it is a power grab.

Forgiving means one gives up the right or the power to punish the other. This is why the offended person will often refuse to listen to the offender's feelings or explanations. To hear her out would be to give some credibility to her point of view and that might mean losing one's power. In this case the offended person is sometimes more interested in the offender not being freed from "responsibility" (actually it's their punishment) than they are about reconciling the matter.

There may be many points at which you feel the weariness of continuing toward your original goal weighing on you. At this point you know there are no guarantees and progress isn't achieved easily, and you know all too well what is involved in rebuilding trust. Nevertheless, to stay mired in hurt and unforgiveness is hopefully not a suitable option. With a note of optimism let me end with the hope you will complete your journey toward rebuilding the trust in your relationship. Now, on we go to finding closure.

CHAPTER SEVENTEEN

Closure the Payoff for Doing the Work

. . . . . .

You have probably heard people speak of the relief of "finding closure" after a hurtful event in their lives. The relief spoken of was most probably that of knowing the event was over in some way and they felt at liberty to move on with their lives. Webster's defines the term closure as, "An often comforting or satisfying sense of finality <victims needing *closure*>; *also*: something (as a satisfying ending) that provides such a sense." For those who have found closure concerning some experience it may have felt as if a heavy weight was laid aside and one was able to sit down, lean back, and rest for a while. To have carried that burden or feel the wound any longer was an unbearable thought. It's a burden no one receiving relief from wants to willingly take up again.

Unfortunately some have carried it for so long it almost seems more natural to have it as a part of life than to be without it. Although repulsed at the thought of picking it up again, some will still return to it for a visit and spend time dwelling on the memories it evokes. This is not a good idea. It is counterproductive to holding onto the closure one has found. I've heard it said, "Never let your past experiences harm your future. Your past can't be altered and your future doesn't deserve the punishment." Once you and I find that sense of closure concerning a past hurt we must hold tightly to it. It is our ticket to a new and better future.

Know What Places Your Closure at Risk

Knowing what puts your sense of closure at risk, or hinders you from finding your closure, will give you the opportunity to avoid that pitfall. The payoff for all the work you have done is at stake. The struggles and pain cannot be allowed to produce nothing more than more struggles and pain. Therefore, consider what could place your closure, or finding it, at risk. Deal with those things and enjoy the payoff.

One of the first things I see threatening people's sense of closure is the idea they have to make sense of the wrong done to them. We can explain and make sense of some events, but not all. The fact is, in your mind, the actions of someone who betrayed you, or failed you, may never be reconciled in your mind. Yet, you can still have closure. Looking back over my own history of hurtful events, I can explain pretty much all of what others did, either psychologically or theologically or with common sense. In some cases, it still doesn't make it all okay because I think, *Yes, but they didn't have to do it. Evidently, in their mind, there was no concern for me.* There's something about being disregarded as irrelevant that bugs me. It strikes at my self-worth. Sure, some of that is ego, but to think that another person can see a human being (you and me) and have no regard for that person—that troubles me. I just cannot afford to allow the offense to own me. I know I have worth even if someone treats me as worthless and therefore I move on with my life.

Next, I see people boxing themselves in by placing expectations on themselves or allowing expectations to be placed on them by others. These folks sometimes have someone in their life saying, "Just get over it!" In annoyance with their advice-giver, I want to tell the person to give their advisor the sarcastic reply of "Well, that's a great idea! That never occurred to me!" Instead, I nicely try to explain to the other person, "It's just not that easy for some people." As is often said to someone experiencing grief, I would say to someone devastated by a breach in trust by a loved one, "Whatever you are feeling is normal," in that someone has felt that way before. It may not be good, but it is usually common to the experience. Hence, there are numerous ways one might experience closure with the same hurt.

Although there are others, the last pitfall I will mention is that of feeling powerless—powerless to forgive, powerless to move on, powerless to control one's feelings—just powerless. By its nature, sometimes the act of someone breaking your trust is uncontrollable. If it had not been, you would have taken control and prevented it. Blaming yourself for not seeing it coming or not preventing it does no good. The events of the past are out of your control. All you have is now and the future. That is all you have hopes of controlling. In spite of this, you and I still cannot control other people. Just the same, the good news is we *can* control ourselves.

In the final analysis, each must make peace with the injury in the way he or she can without the constraints of self-imposed guilt, the expectations of the offender or the onlookers. It is often most beneficial if one can find meaning for one's life, greater self-awareness, a new purpose, renewed strength, a perspective firmly rooted in realistic expectations, the ultimate plan of God, or some other aspect that fosters personal growth and hope for the future. What is to be gained is up to the individual.

You Are Not Powerless

Mark Samuel writes, "Even when you don't have control over the circumstances of a particular situation, you always have a choice over your *reaction* to the situation. You have dominion over your thoughts and your beliefs. You have a choice of what you remember of the situation, over your attitude. That is ultimate power!" If we do not want to feel like a boxer on the ropes taking a merciless beating by the circumstances, we must choose to react, or better yet, *to take action* to deal with the circumstances in the best possible way. Our attitudes will either be the source of our strength or the reason for our demise.

A hopeful, positive attitude is an essential element for formulating a productive response to the circumstances one faces. Otherwise, a person is left to react on an emotional level easily manipulated by the words and actions of others as well as ever-changing circumstances. Perhaps this is one reason some say they feel they are on an emotional rollercoaster. They have no formulated response. At this point all responses are in the moment and driven by external forces. This is a way of living, which perpetuates a sense of being powerless. It can be an agonizing process to reverse. It can feel as if it is purely an exercise of will containing no motivation found in such feelings as hope. Do it anyway. Choose. Choose not to be powerless. Choose a course of action that causes the circumstances to respond to you!

You are the Hero of Your Own Story

Forgiveness and the subsequent closure, which accompanies it, is a result of your actions and your choices. It is always gratifying to hear someone express gratitude for my help in some measure; nevertheless for those who really invest and work to move beyond the events of the past, it is they who deserve the most recognition. They are the heroic ones. As Frederic Luskin, Ph.D. put it, "Forgiveness is the feeling of peace that emerges as you take your hurt less personally, take responsibility for how you feel, and become a hero instead of a victim in the story you tell. Forgiveness is the experience of peacefulness in the present moment. Forgiveness does not change the past, but it changes the present."

This is equally true for the person who has broken the trust of another—wayward spouse, rebellious child, dishonest coworker, abusive parent. Are you tired of being the villain? Would you rather be the hero for once? Write a new story for yourself. Charles R. Swindoll writes,

> Looking back over your shoulder is sometimes a painful experience, especially when you see saddened, shamed, or angry faces. If we were honest with ourselves, we'd admit that the view over our shoulders has too often been a garbage dump when it comes to our relationships. We see the rotten fruit of regrets for things said and not said—a trash bag full of guilt, broken promises, tangled emotions, and non-recyclable pride.

"Looking back over your shoulder" can become a habit that lasts a lifetime if you are not careful. It doesn't have to be that way. The right choices can change it. Do you want to change those memories of "guilt, broken promises, tangled emotions, and non-recyclable pride"? You hold the pen in your hand to write the story you choose. How? Returning to Charles Swindoll's wisdom, "If you want clear away the trash of regret and guilt regarding past relationships, then you must seek forgiveness. And when you do, obey these three commands: start immediately without rationalization, return completely without reservation, and repent openly without hesitation."

Today is a new day. You are, or can become, the hero of your own story and you can write your story any way you choose. Just be clear on this, whether you failed someone or you were failed by someone, it is *your* choice what you become and what you choose to do from here, so write a good story.

What Is It Like to Have Closure?

Closure and forgiveness are fraternal twins. They do not look exactly alike, but often arrive together and have an unbreakable bond. Those who forgive achieve closure. Those who have closure are able to forgive. Forgiveness is more of an action. Closure is more of a feeling.

What is life like for the person who has closure? Each person probably has his/her own list or way of explaining. For me, a few explanations come to mind. Initially, the breach of trust no longer defines oneself, the relationship, or one's participation in the relationship. By this I mean one no longer sees oneself as a victim. Now the person is a survivor. Maybe there is a scar but it reminds the person of the healing and not the pain. The relationship no longer carries a stigma. It doesn't remind the person of bad days, it is now seen in light of being a vehicle for finding more happiness. The individual can plan for the future and dream of the good that can be found.

Next, closure makes itself known through one's ability to extend oneself in relational terms without fear of further hurt taking hold of him or her. Vulnerability is no longer seen as a weakness or a serious risk. The person with closure hopes for new friends, new relationships, and enjoys the ones he or she has been given. No protective shell is needed. Walls have to be torn down and replaced with healthy boundaries.

Finally, closure takes place when "it," whatever "it" is, no longer matters enough to hold on to it. Instead, now we see holding on to it is a worthless use of one's energy. All interest in talking about it has been lost. This is not living in denial. The truth has been realized and addressed. A new reality has been chosen and earned. It is the payoff for doing the hard work.

CHAPTER EIGHTEEN

Closing Thoughts

. . . . . .

E ven now I realize that some who are reading this are yet to be persuaded that they can learn to trust again or even that they want to trust again, if it *were* possible.

In his devotional, *A Psalm in My Heart*, George O. Wood tells the story of an experiment that was captured on film that demonstrated "how adversity may condition us into a state of hopelessness."

> A pike was placed into a large tank. At feeding times minnows (it's favorite food) were poured into the water. The pike energetically swam, gobbling up dinner.
>
> Next, a clear glass cylinder was set in the center of the tank, and the minnows were placed within the oval. Unaware that an invisible wall separated him from his prey, the pike darted for the first minnow—only to slam into the glass. Stunned, he backed away and tried again. Same result.
>
> For a number of hours this process continued. Finally, in defeat, the pike settled to the bottom of the tank.

The glass cylinder was extracted, freeing the
minnows. They swam right by the nose of the pike,
but conditioning had convinced him the minnows were
inaccessible. Eventually he died of starvation.

I can't guarantee you that people will never fail you. I can't
even tell you that you will never be burned again. So, you may be
wondering, "How can I ever learn to trust?" As a parting suggestion I
would encourage taking the time to consider what you stand to gain
by forgiving or lose by not forgiving. Holding on to pain is simply
not worth the many losses one will incur as a result. This is not to
imply the hurt is not important, just that there is more to life than
dwelling on one's past hurts and being emotionally disabled by past
disappointments. Like the pike in the story, far too many people are
emotionally starving to death for love and affection found in healthy
relationships because past experiences have persuaded them to give
up. This is tragic because they have bought into a lie of the most
heartbreaking kind.

Finally, if you are a person of faith, remember that ultimately
God is in control. What does that mean? Read Jeremiah 29:11. It
pretty much says it all, "For I know the thoughts that I think toward
you, says the LORD, thoughts of peace and not of evil, to give you
a future and a hope" (NKJV). God is at work for your good. He
is future oriented in his thinking and planning for you. He deals
in hope and blessings, and nothing and no one can keep Him
from His work in our lives—except us (Romans 8:31-39). If we are
uncooperative and resistant, if we will not walk through the doors of
opportunity He opens for us, and if we refuse to embrace the loving
people He sends into our lives, we are rejecting the future and hope
He is preparing for us.

You Have a Choice

Whether you are the person needing to forgive or be forgiven, both have the same task before them—rebuilding the trust in the relationship. It is important to know and remember you have choices to make and you have a choice of whether or not to make them. You are not powerless unless you choose to be powerless. As I have heard many say, "Whether you believe you can do something or cannot do something, either way you're right." What do you believe?

Additionally I would remind you, although you may have been victimized, *you can choose not to have the mindset of a victim.* When events beyond our control, or choosing, take place in our lives it can be devastating on different levels. These times remind us of how much we can't control, that we are vulnerable, that others do not always reciprocate the same level of commitment to a relationship and we can't make them. We cannot control them no matter how hard we try. Just the same, we can control ourselves.

If you have hurt someone through seriously breaking his or her trust, you can *chose not to be a victimizer.* I say this because I have actually heard people seemingly accepting the false idea that because one or both of their parents had a history of infidelity, or addiction, or divorce for some reason, they too were destined to become like their parents, or just as bad. Because they had failed, it meant they were "that kind of a person" and felt it was not possible for them to be different. "It is what it is," I hear people sometimes say, as a lame way of saying there is nothing that they can do about their situation. Even when we have no control over circumstances we face, many times it ultimately becomes in our minds what we allow it to become and whatever we allow it to be in our minds manifests itself in our lives.

Learn to Value Forgiveness

Many see forgiveness as a tool or a resource for when things go horribly wrong in their lives. Little thought is given to it most days. It will be there when they need it. They know where they keep it—in the back of their minds. Then one day things go wrong and it is taken hold of quickly, and like a man with a new gadget, who won't read the instructions, begins fumbling with it trying to make it work. Eventually he becomes adept at working it for the purpose he needs it to accomplish, but may never know of all its features and capabilities or that he could have been benefiting from its use every day.

In one of my favorite books, *The Power of Personal Accountability*, the authors observe, "Forgiveness is a vacuum cleaner. It can clean cobwebs and dust piles. Use it without moderation. Use it every day. Every time you experience your version of 'the pinch.' It is simple—not easy, but simple. The more you use it the easier it gets." They go on to encourage using forgiveness every day, for example, when we receive inadequate service at a restaurant, in traffic, or at work. Then take one more step, think of something for which you are thankful at that moment. I think pairing the continual use of forgiveness with gratitude helps reinforce letting the small offense go. As for me, I have seen far too many people eaten up with anger, people who appear to despise the world, and appear to see everyone else as dim-witted. They often grow old alone and bitter.

Learning to value forgiveness leads us to being gracious. We have greater empathy. Empathy is compassion and understanding in action. When we are empathetic, we don't just feel sorry for others in crisis, we feel *for* them—we hurt for them. Empathy takes us down to the level of the hurting and causes us to remember when we too hurt, or that but for the grace of God it would be us. We can see ourselves as one who can be hurt or as one who could fail another.

We can clearly see how practicing forgiveness with an empathic and grateful heart would cause us to be better able to forgive when we are deeply hurt.

Perhaps this is why so many self-help or support groups have been started. Someone who had hurt, or failed, or struggled, or mourned said to himself, I want to use my hurt, failure, or struggle to help someone else. Sure, they could have taken care of themselves and moved on with their lives. There's nothing wrong with that. Yet, they found greater meaning and greater healing by continuing to make use of the many functions they have found forgiveness has to offer.

Set Realistic Expectations

When one commits to trusting another, as mentioned previously, expectations must be clear and reasonable. For some it can be difficult to believe that those who are genuinely remorseful are much less likely to fail again. Great sorrow does not necessarily produce self-control or character. Some may still lack self-awareness so much so they truly have difficulty seeing their own faults. On the other side of the coin, some have been so deeply hurt in the past they instinctively strike out in defense at anyone who fails or threatens their sense of well-being, and one can fail to receive forgiveness from that person no matter how sorrowful he or she may be. Good relationships must have realistic expectations. With those expectations set, each can make an informed decision about the future.

In an article titled, *"Rebuilding Trust,"* marriage and family counselor and author Lynette Hoy, writes,

> Trusting another person requires a realistic perspective
> about people and an expectation of failure. Trust needs

to be combined with a willingness to forgive and grows best in an environment of acceptance and love.

There's no magic machine, you don't put in a quarter and out drops a can of trust—trust grows over time. People are complex, broken beings, therefore, previous hurts, fears or losses can impede their determination to trust and/or be truthful in a relationship. But, people have the capacity and the ability to change and to grow in trust and truthfulness. You can rebuild trust in broken relationships when you make a choice to do so with the supernatural help of God.

Retrace the Steps of Your Relationship

Time and healing will produce a better perspective on one's relationship and one's own life, decisions, as well as how one sees oneself.

The fundamentals found in a breach of trust are:

1. *There has to be the belief that a person is trustworthy.* This actually may or may not have any basis in reality. At times people show us multiple examples of their untrustworthy ways and still we ignore them. Still, most of the time we have good reason to believe the person can be trusted. Not everyone is prone to multiple failures in this area.

2. *There is the event that leads to the breaking of the trust in a relationship.* Call it temptation, deceitful behavior, spiteful behavior, an error in judgment, or any other tag one might apply—it nevertheless results in trust being broken.

3. *There is the aftermath.* This is when the revelation of the person's behavior takes place (assuming the person is

forthcoming with an explanation). If there was deceit, it is revealed. If there was poor judgment, it too is discovered. If the temptation was too great for her, or the person was being childish and trying to punish the other person with the trust-breaking behavior, it will become all too clear.

The fundamentals of restoring trust are found by reversing the order of the previous path to breaking trust:

1. *The person who has lost the trust of another is allowed to become a person who openly addresses his or her feelings and struggles without being penalized for it.* There must be the genuine hope in the person's heart he or she will be able to be trusted again. Holding past failures over another's head only guarantees the destruction of that relationship. In return for the hope, he or she will also take steps to ensure there is a way of escape when confronted with temptation, do nothing that might be perceived as deceitful, clear boundaries of acceptable behavior with himself/herself, and others will be adopted, and overall takes a wiser approach to living one's life.

2. *When temptation comes or a situation ripe for failure presents itself, the person in question is proactive in protecting himself from failing and in protecting his or her relationship.* This is done by removing himself from the situation, calling an accountability partner, or by sticking to the boundaries previously set. No justifying. No rationalizing. No doing what one wants out of rebellion or spite for something said or done or because one is angry the other person hasn't dropped the whole subject. There are more people to prove oneself trustworthy than the person with whom one is

angry. Maybe the most needed is the proving to oneself one is trustworthy.

3. *Trust will begin to grow in the heart and mind of the person who was originally betrayed.* That person will be able to see clear examples of trustworthy behavior, not to mention the commitment required to maintain that behavior. This will become the basis for that person trusting again. Time and commitment will bring healing. Flashbacks will usually go away eventually. A new normal will develop and it can be a good normal. Having survived, the relationship will have a greater bond and a deeper love.

Lay a Good Foundation

- Rebuilding requires a good look at our foundation because where and how we choose to begin at this point will make an enormous difference. Previously, had we built on poorly laid foundations we thought were solid relationships or with people we thought solid, only to realize that they had consistently revealed their true nature to us and yet we refused to see? Questions about our foundation must be asked before we rebuild with confidence. Questions like: Did we trust the relationship to stand the test of time when we had done little to support or build it up?

- How could we have made the foundation stronger? Were our expectations of others realistic?

- Did we fail to connect with the other person in the past?

- We know they were not genuine at some point. What about us?

- Where and in whom do we place our trust where we won't be disappointed?

You've probably seen the sign in a store before that says, "In God we trust; all others pay cash." That's seems to be the philosophy of many in our society. They say, "I don't trust anyone but God." But do they really even trust God? What happened to believing that God can lead, guide, and direct us in our lives? What happened to believing that God is looking out for us? In my experience, placing my faith in God has taught me a great deal about trusting someone besides myself, as well as the expectations of commitment in a relationship. It's too easy as humans to fall into the trap of cynicism and decide we will trust no one but ourselves. The problem I found with that philosophy is that I am so very limited. Yes, I have been deeply hurt and disappointed by some people. I have the scars. I also have the realization I need relationships with other people and a relationship with my Creator. With that realization and truth in mind, I can confidently say, when it is possible, I believe rebuilding the trust in a relationship is worth the effort.

APPENDIX

Exercise

Relationship Trust Agreement

......

I mportant: *The purpose of an agreement of this type is purely educational and meant only to clarify the needs and expectations of those involved, to remove areas of misunderstandings, and to bring to light unspoken needs. It is to be used as a tool for drawing closer to one another and nothing more. Ideally, in every relationship where trust is an issue, those involved could come up with their own version that is uniquely appropriate for them. (Examples: previous infidelity, drug or alcohol use, anger issues—where there is no physical danger, etc.) Use this as a guide if you think it could be useful.*

_____ and _____ agree to commit ourselves to take the necessary steps to build and/or rebuild the trust in our relationship to preserve and nurture our relationship as specified by the following:

I _____ understand that ultimately I must make a choice to believe in the trustworthiness of _____ and to commit myself to being supportive, understanding, and

Mark Beaird

gracious of him/her in order to help him/her to feel comfortable in investing more and more of himself/herself in our relationship. In return,   , understands that in order for me to believe that I and our relationship are being respected and that I can place my trust securely in him/her, I need the following from _____:

_____

_____

_____

I _____ understand that ultimately I must make a choice to believe in the trustworthiness of _____ and to commit myself to being supportive, understanding, and gracious of him/her in order to help him/her to feel comfortable in investing more and more of himself/herself in our relationship. In return, _____ understands that in order for me to believe that I and our relationship are being respected and that I can place my trust securely in him/her, I need the following from _____:

_____

_____

_____

Essentials for _____ are:

Essentials for _____ are:

This agreement is approved by us with the understanding that *this agreement is to only be used as a reference for expectations and needs with the intent of building a bond of trust in our relationship* and *not as a means of penalizing the other or keeping score.* With the anticipation of developing a deeper bond in our relationship, the undersigned agree to acknowledge and respect what has been shared with him/her by his/her spouse.

_____ and

_____

Date: _____

WORKS CITED

Baucom, D. H., Snyder, D. K., and Gordon, K. C., Helping Couples Get Past the Affair: A Clinicians Guide. Guilford. (2009)

Baylor, Helen, "5 Minutes With Helen Baylor." *Today's Christian Woman* 22.1 (2000): 59. *MasterFILE Premier.* Web. 15 Oct. 2012.

Beck, A. T., (1976) *Cognitive therapies and emotional disorders.* New York: New American Library.

Bagarozzi, D. A., (2008) Understanding and Treating Marital Infidelity: A Multidimensional Model. *American Journal Of Family Therapy,* 36 (1), 1-17.

Beam, Joe. (2012) *The Art of Falling in Love.* Howard Books. New York

Bernstein, Albert, *Emotional Vampires: Dealing with People Who Drain You Dry.* New York:McGraw-Hill, 2001. 242 pages.

Blow, A. J., (2005) Face it head on: Helping a couple move through the painful and pernicious effects of infidelity. *The Journal of Couple and Relationship Therapy,* 4, 91-102.

Blow, A. J., (2008, March/April) "Key considerations for clinicians working with couples and infidelity." *Family Therapy Magazine,* 12-14.

Brant, Mary Jane Hurley, *Loyalty Vs. Blind Loyalty In Families.* 2012 Patch http://radnor.patch.com/articles/loyalty-vs-blind-loyalty-in-families.

Burns, D. D., (1980) *Feeling good: The new mood therapy.* New York: New American Library.

Carder, Dave, (2008) *Torn Assunder: Recovery from Extramarital Affairs.* Moody Publishers, Revised edition.

Carnes, Patrick J. Ph.D., (2001) *Out of the Shadows: Understanding Sexual Addiction* Hazelden; MN Third Edition edition.

Cloud, Henry and Townsend, John (1995), *Safe People: How to Find Relationships That Are Good for You and Avoid Those That Aren't.* Zondervan.

Cloud, H. A., *Boundaries: When to Say Yes, How to Say No to Take Control of Your Life.* (Grand Rapids: Zondervan 2002).

Cloud-Townsend (July 27, 2000), Cloud-Townsend Resources Integrity Outlines

By Henry Cloud, Ph.D., Copyright © 2000 Cloud-Townsend Resources, All rights reserved.

http://www.cloudtownsend.com/integrity-outlines/trust/.

Collingwood, Jane (2008), "Trust and Vulnerability in Relationships." *Psych Central.* Retrieved on December 6, 2012, from http://psychcentral.com/lib/2008/trust-and-vulnerability-in-relationships.

Coleman, Joshua, The Greater Good Science Center at the University of California, Berkeley. (2012) http://greatergood.berkeley.edu/article/item/surviving_betrayal/#. Accessed 12/6/12.

Covey, Stephen. SPEED of Trust: The One Thing that Changes Everything. http://www.tipsonlifeandlove.com/your-money-and-career/inspiring-trust#ixzz2Bkx2dVCv.

Crane, Frank, Brainy Quote (2001-2012) BrainyQuote. Accessed 10/22/12   http://www.brainyquote.com/quotes/quotes/f/ frankcrane163038.html

Davis, D. E., Hook, J. N., Worthington Jr., E. L., Van Tongeren, D. R., Gartner, A. L., Ii, D., and Emmons, R. A. (2011), "Relational Humility: Conceptualizing and Measuring Humility as a Personality Judgment." *Journal Of Personality Assessment, 93*(3), 225-234. doi:10.1080/00223891.2011.558871

Dimoka, A. (2010), "What Does the Brain Tell Us about Trust and Distrust? Evidence from a Functional Neuroimaging Study." *MIS Quarterly, 34*(2), 373-A7.

Draper, Edythe, *Draper's Book of Quotations for the Christian World* (Wheaton: Tyndale House Publishers, Inc., 1992). Entries 2183-2186.

Fehr, R., and Gelfand, M. J. (2009), "But I Said I Was Sorry! On the Importance of Matching Apologies to Victim Self-Construals." *Academy of Management Annual Meeting Proceedings*, 1-6.

Fenell, D. L. (1993), "Characteristics of long-term first marriages." *Journal of Mental Health Counseling, 15, 446-460.*

Ferch, Shann R., "Intentional Forgiving as a Counseling Intervention." *Journal of Counseling and Development,* 07489633, Summer 98, Vol. 76, Issue 3.

Gottman, John M. and Silver, Nan (1999), *Seven Principles for Making Marriage Work*, Three Rivers Press

Gottman, John, (2011). *The Science of Trust: Emotional Attunement for Couples.* W. W. Norton and Company, New York, NY

Grohol, J. M., *PsychCentral.* Retrieved February 1, 2011, from Psychcentral.com: http://psychcentral.com/lib/2009/ fixing-cognitive-distortions/.

Grohol, J. (2009), 15 Common Cognitive Distortions. *Psych Central.* Retrieved on November 26, 2012, from http://psychcentral. com/lib/2009/15-common-cognitive-distortions/

Hargrave, PhD., Terry D., "Forgiveness and Reconciliation after Infidelity." *Family therapy Magazine.* March-April 2008, p 30-33

Hargrave, T. D. (2001), *Forgiving the devil: Healing damaged relationships.* Phoenix: Zeig, Tucker and Theisen.

Holy Bible, New King James Version (NKJV) Copyright © 1982 by Thomas Nelson, Inc.

Holy Bible, New International Version, (NIV) Copyright © 1973, 1978, 1984, 2011 by Biblica, Inc.

Holy Bible. New Living Translation (NLT) copyright© 1996, 2004, 2007 by Tyndale House Foundation. Used by permission of Tyndale House Publishers Inc., Carol Stream, Illinois 60188. All rights reserved.

Hoy, Lynette (2012), "Rebuilding Trust." http://powertochange. com/discover/sex-love/rebuildtrust/ Power to Change Ministries. Accessed 10/15/12.

Kent M. Keith—http://www.goodreads.com/quotes/tag/honesty.

Kiefer, R. P., Worthington, E. L., Myers, B. J., Kliewer, W. L., Berry, J. W., Davis, D. E., and Hunter, J. L. (2010), "Training Parents in Forgiving and Reconciling." *American Journal Of Family Therapy, 38*(1), 32-49. doi:10.1080/01926180902945723.

Kirshenbaum, Mira. *I Love You But I Don't Trust You: The Complete Guide to Restoring Trust in Your Relationship.*

Kübler-Ross, E. (1969), *On Death and Dying,* Routledge.

Lansky, D., (accessed November 30, 2012) "Three Attributes of Trust." Family Business Wisdom, Thoughts and Education. http:// efamilybusiness.com.

Lucado, Max, http://mattkinger.tumblr.com/post/6552363620/ max-lucado-i-will-not-abandon-you. Accessed_12/1/12.

Luskin, F. (2002), *Forgive for good: a proven prescription for health and happiness*. New York: HarperSan Francisco.

May, Bernie, (1985) *Learning to Trust*, Multnomah Press.

May, L. N., and Jones, W. H. (2007), "Does Hurt Linger? Exploring the Nature of Hurt Feelings over Time." *Current Psychology*, 25(4), 245-256.

Mayer, R. C., Davis, J. H., and Schoorman, F. D. 1995. "An Integrative Model of Organizational Trust," *Academy of Management Review* (20:3), pp. 709-734.

Mayer, J. D., Caruso, D., and Salovey, P. (1999), "Emotional intelligence meets traditional standards for an intelligence." *Intelligence, 27*, 267-298.

Mayo Clinic, "Forgiveness: Letting go of grudges and bitterness." Mayo Clinic staff Original Article: http://www.mayoclinic.com/health/forgiveness/MH00131 MH00131 Nov. 23, 2011. Accessed 11/16/12

McBurney, M.D., Louis. (1992). "Avoiding Threats to Your Relationship." Focus on the Family. Retrieved on December 18, 2012 from http://www.focusonthefamily.com/marriage/preparing_for_marriage/approaching_the_wedding_day/avoiding_threats_to_your_marriage.aspxMoore, K.A., Chalk, R., Scarpa, J., and Vandivere, S. (2002, August), *Family strengths: Often overlooked, but real*. (Washington, DC: Child Trends).

Morrow, Lance, (1986). *The Chief: A Memoir of Fathers and Sons*. (Collier Books Collier Macmillan Canada, Incorporated).

Murphy, Stacy Notaras. "What becomes of the brokenhearted?" *Counseling Today*. November 2012—Vol. 55/number 5 P.40-43.

McGregor, D., *The Professional Manager*. (New York: McGraw-Hill, 1967). p 163.

McLeod, Carolyn, "Trust," *The Stanford Encyclopedia of Philosophy (Spring 2011 Edition)*, Edward N. Zalta (ed.), URL = <http://plato.stanford.edu/archives/spr2011/entries/trust/>. Accessed

Orloff, Judith, (2011) *Emotional Freedom: Liberate Yourself From Negative Emotions and Transform Your Life.* (Three Rivers Press). New York, NY

Orloff, Judith, *Who's the Emotional Vampire in Your Life.* Dr. Judith Orloff's Blog. http://www.drjudithorloff.com/_blog/Dr_Judith_Orloff's_Blog/post/Who's_the_Emotional_Vampire_in_Your_Life/. Accessed 11/18/12.

Otto, Jean—Edythe Draper, *Draper's Book of Quotations for the Christian World* (Wheaton: Tyndale House Publishers, Inc., 1992). Entries 2797-2798.

Nelson, M. B. (2000), *The Unburdened Heart: 5 keys to forgiveness and freedom.* (New York: Harper San Francisco).

Righetti, Francesca; Finkenauer, Catrin, "If you are able to control yourself, I will trust you: The role of perceived self-control in interpersonal trust." *Journal of Personality and Social Psychology, Vol 100(5),* May 2011, 874-886.

Sadlier, Dan, "Faithfulness vs. Loyalty"—July 23, 2012. http://www.dansadlier.com/2012/07/faithfulness-vs-loyalty/. Accessed 10/22/12.

Samuel, Mark. and Chiche, Sophie, *The Power of Personal Accountability: Achieve what matters to you.* (Katonah, NY: Xephor Press 2004).

Smedes, Lewis B., (1984) *FORGIVE and FORGET.* (Harper and Row).

Smedes, Lewis, "Five Things Everyone Should Know about Forgiving"

Program #4101 First air date October 5, 1997. http://www.30goodminutes.org/csec/sermon/smedes_4101.htm.

Snyder, D. K., Baucom, D. H., and Gordon, K. C. (2007), "Treating infidelity: An integrative approach to resolving trauma and promoting forgiveness." In P. Peluso (Ed.) *Infidelity: A practitioner's guide to working with couples in crisis* (pp. 99-125). (Philadelphia: Routledge).

Swindoll, Charles R (2001 and Message Mate 2008), *Insight for Living series: Committed to Excellence in Communicating Biblical Truth and Its Application.* Insight for Living, Plano, TX

The Center for Parenting Education—Staff writers. (2006-2012) *When Your Teen Breaks Your Trust.* Accessed 11/15/12. http://www.centerforparentingeducation.org/programs_articlesresource_teens_trust.html.

Twain, Mark, *Following the Equator*, Pudd'nhead Wilson's New Calendar http://www.twainquotes.com/Experience.html.

Merriam-Webster, I. *Merriam-Webster's Collegiate Dictionary, 11th Edition.* (Merriam-Webster, Inc. 2008).

Merriam-Webster Online Dictionary copyright © 2012 by Merriam-Webster, Incorporated http://www.merriam-webster.com/dictionary/closure.

Vaz, Louella, "Building trust in relationships." FutureScopes. http://futurescopes.com. Accessed November 29, 2011.

Wilson, S. (2012), What's His Is Ours. *Christianity Today, 56*(8), 32.

Wikipedia "For Want of a Nail." http://en.wikipedia.org/wiki/For_Want_of_a_Nail accessed 12/6/12.

Wood, George O(1997), *A Psalm in my heart. Springfield, MO:* (Gospel Publishing House).

RECOMMENDED READING BY CATEGORY

· · · · · ·

Personal improvement

Burns, D. D. (1980), *Feeling good: The new mood therapy.* (New York: New American Library).

The Power of Personal Accountability

Holy Bible, New International Version, (NIV) Copyright © 1973, 1978, 1984, 2011 by Biblica, Inc.

Seligman, M. E., *Learned Optimism: How to Change Your Mind and Your Life.* Knopf, (New York 1991: Paperback reprint edition, Penguin Books, 1998; reissue edition, Free Press, 1998).

Samuel, Mark and. Chiche, Sophie *The Power of Personal Accountability: Achieve what matters to you.* (Katonah, NY: Xephor Press 2004).

Forgiveness

Lewis B. Smedes, *FORGIVE & FORGET.* 1984, (Harper and Row).

Nelson, M. B. (2000). *The Unburdened Heart: 5 keys to forgiveness and freedom.* (New York: Harper).

Infidelity

Joe Beam, 2012. *The Art of Falling in Love.* (New York: Howard Books).

Carder Dave, (2008) *Torn Assunder: Recovery from Extramarital Affairs.* (Moody Publishers, Revised Edition)

Relationship Improvement

Gottman, John, *Making Marriage Work* (Audio version can be found on iTunes)

Gottman, John. (2011), *The Science of Trust: Emotional Attunement for Couples.* (New York, NY: W. W. Norton & Company).

Gottman, J.M. and Silver, N, *Why Marriages Succeed or Fail.* (New York: Simon and Schuster, 1994).

Stanley, Scott, (2005). *The Power of Commitment: A Guide to Lifelong Love.* (San Francisco, CA: Jossy-Bass).

Townsend and Cloud, *Safe People.*

Townsend and Cloud, *Boundaries in Marriage.*

Townsend and Cloud, *Boundaries: When to say yes and when to say no.*

Relationships with Difficult People

Bernstein, Albert, *Emotional Vampires: Dealing with People who Drain you Dry.* (New York: McGraw-Hill, 2001). 242 pages.

Twenge, Jean, Campbell, Keith, (2009) *The Narcissism Epidemic: Living in the age of entitlement.* New York. Free Press.

Troublesome Issues

Patrick J. Carnes Ph.D., *Out of the Shadows: Understanding Sexual Addiction* (Hazelden; MN) Third Edition, May 23, 2001. (Anything by this author on the subject of addictions is worth reading.)

I Hate You—Don't Leave Me: Understanding the Borderline Personality by Jerold J. Kreisman, MD, and Hal Straus. (New York: Penguin Group USA Inc., 2010).

Beyond Anger: A Guide For Men: How To Free Yourself From The Grip of Anger and Get More Out Of Life, by Thomas Harbin.

Online Sources for Articles

www.mayoclinic.com
www.webmd.com
www.mjhb.net
www.helpguide.org

ABOUT THE AUTHOR

......

Mark Beaird, MA
Licensed Professional Counselor
Nationally Certified Counselor
Certified Alcohol and Drug Counselor
Internationally Certified Alcohol and Drug Counselor

Mark started out as a pastor and after several years realized his passion was pastoral care or caring for the needs of the hurting. With all the pastoral counseling required in his work it was a natural transition into the field of professional counseling. His work as a counselor focuses mainly on marriage and relationship improvement, as well as mood disorders and life transitions. Mark has also done work as a columnist and freelance writer and has been published in various newspapers and periodicals around the country. He has also authored several other books, mainly in the devotional and inspirational genres.

Presently Mark continues to work as a therapist and life coach and to continue his writing. He and his wife Elaine have been married for thirty years and have two daughters.

For more information or articles or to contact Mark visit him on the web at www.markbeaird.org.

CPSIA information can be obtained
at www.ICGtesting.com
Printed in the USA
LVOW11s1740081017
551667LV00001B/51/P